# Confessions of a Local Government Officer

## Peter M Kitchen

Photographs by the author

With thanks to all contributors.

Every care has been taken in compiling this publication to provide accurate information.

Copyright © 2008 by Peter M Kitchen

ISBN-13: 978-1-4092-4947-4

## CONTENTS

1 EARLY YEARS — 1

2 THE NINETEEN SEVENTIES — 30

3 THE EARLY NINETEEN EIGTIES — 51

4 THE ADVENT OF THE PC — 72

5 THE NINETEEN NINETIES — 93

6 THE TWENTY FIRST CENTURY — 112

7 RECENT EVENTS — 123

8 THE FUTURE — 142

# 1

## EARLY YEARS

This is one man's account of the changes in the way of life over the last forty to fifty years.

This in particular relates to those that have happened over that period in the offices at Lancashire County Council in Preston – especially in the use of computers and in education. I'm sure it could apply to work places anywhere. I wouldn't have believed when I started its resemblance to a soap opera!

Many changes have been for the better others decidedly questionable.

I have recounted amusing stories, whenever I could remember them. These are both first hand and others that friends and colleagues have told me about. Whenever I have referred to anyone, his or her name has been changed. I have always tried to provide correct information but must apologise for any inaccuracies.

Most remarkable are the everyday changes that have just happened without anyone being aware of them. Many of these will only be apparent to those of us over fifty. Until the late 1960s they took place only very slowly – families buying washing machines, fridges, becoming car owners and obtaining a telephone for the first time.

Colour TVs began to appear. A reporter on the radio was explaining to her son that 40 years ago people only had a black and white television. At first he just seemed to be incredulous but that changed to 'Don't be so stupid mother!'

In the early days of television a colleague's grandfather had told his daughter that they had bought a colour television set. The whole family went round in great expectation to discover a black and white box with three strips of cellophane over the screen. Blue at the top for the sky, reddish brown in the centre for the buildings and green at the bottom for the grass! Technology well ahead of its time!

It's hard to believe now that to change channels you had to rotate a dial to 2 for BBC and to 9 for ITV. Broadcasting closed down at 11pm leaving nothing to see on the screen but a test card. When the first remote controls appeared people that possessed one were regarded as too lazy and stupid for words. To not even have to get up from the settee to alter the volume was regarded as the height of sloth!

In 1969, the year that I left the sixth form, I had a summer job working at GEM, a supermarket that later was replaced by ASDA. Whilst shopping there with my parents in May, I enquired if there were any jobs going for the school holidays. 'Sure, when can you start?' was the answer. I told him three weeks on Monday. 'Right, be there for 8 o'clock'!

That was the interview. I don't think that he even took a note of my name or age. It was easy come easy go at that time. If I didn't turn up nobody would have even noticed.

I sat my last A level on a Friday morning in early June at Preston Grammar School. Following that exam, we shook hands with the teacher who wished us all the best and said that it had been nice knowing us and we left. There was no such thing as a leaving ceremony or school ball that are popular nowadays. We all went our separate ways to our temporary summer jobs, awaiting our exam results in mid August.

In today's world we have hypermarkets on the outskirts of all major towns, retail parks with DIY stores, giant furniture, toy and clothes shops. At that time a supermarket was very much a novelty. The nearest thing to it had been the neighbourhood co-ops or large grocery shops such as Booths in the High Street. This town centre store, shown below, closed in the nineteen-eighties.

GEM was the first large supermarket in the area, being located in an old mill in Ribbleton with plenty of car parking but within easy walking distance of thousands of homes and with a free bus service every half hour from Lancaster Road in the town centre.

I did arrive at 8 am that Monday. It was a huge shock to someone who'd been cosseted in an academic background for years. At school nobody would even dare to risk being overheard using a word such as 'damn.' Here the norm for most staff was to use the f word at least once in every sentence in a manner that would surprise Gordon Ramsey. Another jolt to the system was how many employees at the younger end found excuses to completely avoid working if at all possible.

I handed in my NI card and received a clocking-in card. Anyone who was more than two minutes late clocking in was docked quarter of an hours pay. Jobs consisted of unloading lorries, transferring goods from them to the conveyor belt, loading them on to pallets, stacking them in the warehouse, individually pricing the boxes and taking them upstairs to the shop. Early in the week there was a procession of vehicles, queuing to be unloaded. Four tons of sugar would arrive, followed by crates of heavy tinned fruit or pet foods. A load of light biscuits came as a relief.

A one-off job that had to be done was to put new price labels on the boxes of all goods that had a half penny in the price, in preparation for the coin being removed from the currency that August. That was in old money of course. Almost always a price such as 1/1½d became 1/2d. In the food hall any alteration to a price had to be changed on each item in the box.

In the same casual manner that staff were taken on, employment could be terminated. One youth stuck his foot out to trip up a weaker lad. In the manner of Alan Sugar's 'The Apprentice' he was instantly told by the warehouse manager 'You're fired'. I discovered later that each summer they got rid of many of the permanent staff that they regarded as thugs, to be replaced by students. They then had another recruitment drive in September.

Staff were allowed to buy damaged tins at reduced prices. One popular trick was to take the label of a can of steak, knock a dint into it and then say to the man in charge of the warehouse 'Can I have this spoiled tin of cat food for half price?'

The check-outs were a long way removed from those of today, where bar codes are read by a laser. Every single item was individually priced and the amount entered into the comptometer. This was a slow process. Regularly eight or ten trolley loads were waiting at the tills. The fact that you could go shopping until eight o'clock at night on Wednesdays to Fridays – at least two hours after most grocery shops had closed made the wait in the queue and the expedition worthwhile.

Everyone lined up to receive their pay in cash in a little wage packet envelope on Fridays. The maximum weekly pay was £14 and 14 shillings when you were 22. Customers also paid for their purchases in cash. There was no such thing as credit or debit cards. The use of a cheque book wasn't commonplace. Even several years later paying by cheques was quite a hassle. Your cheque guarantee card would only accept one for at most £30. One person buying some hi-fi equipment in Boots chemist costing £65 had to write out three separate cheques with a different date written onto each one before they would be accepted. The only other method of buying things such as a sofa was to pay by hire purchase. This would entail going into the shop and making a payment each month. Many people were very snobbish about hire purchase or the never-never and used to pass snide comments about their neighbours – 'I bet she's only bought that on HP!'

Until a few years before the co-operative stores located in many of the urban areas had operated a system of dividends. Each time that you went into the shop the amount that you had purchased was written onto a label which you stuck onto a sheet known as a 'gum sheet'. There was room for about twenty of these per sheet. When it was full the person behind the counter had to add up all the entries. This was long before the days of calculators and was in pounds, shillings and pence. The shop assistant was expected to total them with nothing more than a pencil and paper. You then received a shilling for every pound spent. Perhaps this should be introduced into GCSE mathematics.

After the initial shock I felt that I learnt far more about people and life, was much stronger and worldlier from those three months in the supermarket than from all the previous years at Preston Grammar School. Unloading crates of beans all morning was far more beneficial that a workout at a gym. Sadly I have few happy memories from that school. Many years before I used to think it was an establishment for old people 'Preston Grandma's School!' Staff were called 'masters' rather than teachers. They taught in their gowns much as they had done in the 1930s when my father had attended. Many gave out impositions for such trivial offences as getting a low mark in a test or to the whole form because someone made a noise going into the classroom. These varied from writing out 100 times 'I must not make a noise entering class' to copying out 40 verses from Psalm 119 in the bible! Rather than study a section from a book or learn French vocabulary because they were interesting or you might benefit, you learnt them to avoid having to copy two pages of meaningless text if you did not get a sufficiently high mark in the next assessment.

Nowadays the focus of schools is based on health,

enjoyment and achievement, contributing to society, economic well-being and feeling safe. Schools are inspected and reported upon how well they perform under these headings. The Grammar School was anything but safe. Bullying by teachers and pupils was regarded as grounding for when you left. No-one could ever approach a member of staff to talk about a problem. Humiliation and sarcasm were more popular. If a pupil was asked a question and didn't know the answer the teacher's pet was instructed 'Tell him, Kershaw.' On one occasion, even in the 6th form, a student went to the staff room to take some work and asked to see a member of staff. The teacher answering the door called his colleague and said 'Mr Thornthwaite there's a child come to see you.' You were expected to stand up when you spoke to a teacher. One pupil who remained seated was told 'Stand up when you speak to the oracle and ventilate your brain!'

Some teachers in fits of temper threw wooden board dusters. One hit a pupil on his forehead, resulting in a gush of blood. Bearing in mind what happened to Goliath this could have had disastrous consequences. Nowadays he would, quite rightly, be charged with assault. In those days nothing happened whatsoever. No-one would dare report it for fear of receiving a thick ear or other penalty and being told that he must have deserved it.

One teacher who taught French used to make pupils do press-ups as a punishment. Another used a long fold-up ruler as a cane. Before using the implement he once said to his victim 'Forehand or backhand? But I might warn you that I'm an expert at both!'

Another instructed everyone to back their text books with brown paper. The following day each pupil's books were inspected. He commented that one boy had backed it very well. The teacher then hit someone who was talking on the back of his head with the book. Unsurprisingly it fell to bits and the lad to whom it belonged was told that he hadn't backed it properly.

An anachronism in the school was known as the 'Bulling board'. When the headmaster had caned someone their name and details were put onto a notice board. A typical entry might read 'Johnson of 5B and of Miller House has been beaten for gross discourtesy to a member of staff.' One pupil had tried to start a fire in class. The caning notice stated 'Barnes of 4C and of Thornley house has been beaten for trying to set the school on fire – not for lack of success!'

Whilst someone who was very gifted academically or had sporting ability benefited greatly from the regime, those of us with less talents did not. The fact that the sports ground was almost three miles from school necessitating a trek with a satchel full of books for homework and a duffel bag containing sports kit followed by an inconvenient bus journey into town afterwards was a considerable deterrent.

I was told many years after leaving, when chatting to someone who had previously taught at the school, that a lot of the staff did not care for the headmaster or the way in which he ran the school. One tale that I recall relates to a physics teacher who used to brew beer adjacent to the laboratory. Whilst the form was waiting to go into the room on one occasion the headmaster could smell the aroma and said to the teacher 'Mr Bell, I can smell beer on one of your boys.' 'Nay, that'll be mine brewing in the dark room!' Later the Head had a quiet word with the teacher. 'You realise I can have you dismissed for this'. He retorted 'Listen, if I go most of this physics lab goes with me!'

When I reached the 6th form the school no longer took first year pupils, becoming entirely a sixth form college five years later. The Girls Grammar School further along Moor Park Avenue (The Park School) changed similarly. Staff and students from both schools later moved to a purpose built tertiary college in Fulwood, known initially as Tuson College, named after a former chief education officer, later changing to Preston College.

The grammar school buildings were used by two high schools called Northlands and Parklands. These subsequently merged to become Moor Park High School. In the days of specialist schools it is now known as 'Moor Park Business and Enterprise College.'

The former Park School on Moor Park Avenue.

Whilst like many people I have great concerns about the behaviour of children, their lack of respect and the feeling of being powerless to be able to do anything about it, I was glad nevertheless to see the demise of Preston Grammar School and its methods of imposing discipline.

On the fringe of the town centre there were two catholic grammar schools – the Catholic College for boys and Lark Hill Convent for girls. A new comprehensive school in Penwortham replaced them. The boys school became a sixth form college for boys and girls, Cardinal Newman College. The old buildings were sold and Newman moved into the premises of the former Lark Hill.

The two other grammar schools in the Preston area met different destinies. Kirkham Grammar became a private fee paying school whilst Hutton Grammar continued to provide education for 11 to 18 year old boys and retained its name.

Although it became comprehensive in nature much of the ethos of its former days was retained and it was and still is a popular choice for pupils around the town. In the 1980s girls were also admitted to the sixth form.

It is fascinating to look at some of the vast changes since the nineteen-sixties.

One of these was access to music. Today with dozens of radio channels and iPods that fit in your pocket and may hold 15,000 songs or tunes is a million miles from the 1960s where a 45 rpm vinyl single lasting two or three minutes cost 6/8d (33p) well over an hour's wages for a typical eighteen year old. The main source of pop music was Radio Luxembourg which only switched on at about 7 o'clock in the evening. Reception was so bad in the summer as to make listening impossible. I'm sure that I wasn't the only youngster to sneak the transistor radio under the bed sheets late at night! Even more remarkable was that most programmes could only play music on a specific record label. If my memory is correct the popular Teens and Twenties disc club hosted by Jimmy Saville could only play music on the Decca label – OK for Elvis Presley but would exclude the Beatles on Parlophone, part of the EMI group.

The highlight of the week was Alan Freeman's 'Pick of the Pops' on Sunday afternoons on the Light Programme. Some new releases were played followed by the top ten. Reception could be guaranteed.

In the mid 1960s 'Top of the Pops' on TV was a great boost along with the pirate radio stations Radio Caroline and London. This was to have a huge impact on the BBC to restructure broadcasting to form the new station of Radio 1 (predominantly pop), Radio 2 replacing the Light programme, Radio 3 the Third programme and Radio 4 the Home Service.

This time marked the end of an era on the streets. In each long terraced road there was always the sight of housewives proudly polishing their step. The familiar appearance of a rag and bone man pushing his cart and calling out 'raa-boh' in the neighbourhood was disappearing. What did you get in return for giving a few rags? A lump of soapstone to polish some more steps! The weekly deliveries of bags of coal – the 'coalman' with his sacks were rapidly vanishing as families increasingly had central heating and gas fires fitted.

There seemed to be a sweet shop on every corner with a chewing gum machine that dispensed an extra packet every four turns when the arrow was pointing towards you. People bought bottles of pop with a 3d deposit that was returned to you when you brought back the empty bottle. Of course there was invariably the cigarette machine outside the shop with Woodbines, Senior Service and Capstan full strength. Packets of five could be purchased inside the shop and many shopkeepers would sell individual cigarettes and a few matches to children! A sweet shop and tobacconist just up the road from us was next door to the Empress cinema. In addition to the usual items for sale the proprietor ran a private library from it.

Every Saturday afternoon the cinema showed a matinee for kids. Dozens of children, from eight year old upwards, queued waiting for it to open. Nobody was dropped off or picked up by their parents in those days. We all made our own way there. Entrance to the pictures was 6d and we used to spend 2d or 3d on a lucky bag at the adjacent shop. The programme used to consist of slap stick comedy with the Three Stooges. This was invariably followed by the Pathe News ending with the main film - a cowboy.

Sundays were normally very boring days with not much happening. The only shops that were open were newsagents and those selling sweets. Lots of us had to go to Sunday school where we were given grounding about stories from the bible. I think that the sole purpose was to get us from under our parents' feet for an hour.

St David's church hall where we had to attend Sunday School every weekend

If it was a scorching hot day the family would have a trip to the seaside with grandparents tagging along. Although the journey to Blackpool was less than twenty miles it is hard to credit what an effort it was at that time. You had to get the bus into town and then trudge along to the train station. All the youngsters would be accompanied by their buckets and spades. Eventually you'd arrive and make you way to the beach. Deck chairs were obtained and fathers would roll up the bottoms of their trousers and place a knotted handkerchief over their head to keep out the sun in exactly the manner of the saucy postcards. Most of them still wore their jacket but they might loosen their tie! The best part of the day was the trip to Roberts Oyster Bar in the evening for a plate of cockles. It was then back to the station for the long queue for the train home.

Lots of families had a vacation at a guest house in a seaside resort during wakes week. The whole town shut down. Every shop in the town centre was closed for the period. Foreign holidays were unknown.

One thing above all that has changed is kids playing out. Against every wall children used to throw two balls repeatedly against it with two hands or one handed. Many school girls almost lived upside down, the amount of time that was spent doing hand stands or cart wheeling across the road. Every youngster in the neighbourhood played hopscotch and games such as aunties and uncles where everyone stood on a back line. A caller would shout out a name such as James or Linda. If you had an uncle or aunt by that name you leapt forward as far as you could. The winner was the first person to reach the front line. Some parents must have had twenty brothers and sisters the rate at which some children arrived at the winning line! There was always the sight of skipping ropes with a person holding each end and a couple jumping over the rope together to a rhyme such as 'Jelly on the plate, jelly on the plate, wibble wobble, wibble wobble, jelly on the plate.' After ten minutes the ropes were exchanged for hoola hoops.

All the pupils in the class had hobbies. Fishing, football, train spotting and stamp collecting were the most popular. You could buy packets containing dozens of the most widely available foreign stamps for 6d at Woolworths. We used to swap them in class before assembly. Fishing was very much a 'Dads and Lads' activity. Dozens spent many an evening on the canal bank with a rod and line as did their fathers. The youngest kids took sticks with a little net on the end to the pond to catch sticklebacks and minnows – tiddlers as they used to call them. Most Saturday afternoons in the summer I used to catch the Ribble bus with my father to Catforth carrying fishing tackle, a basket and even a little seat. Although the journey was only about four miles, the destination was completely rural and totally different from the urban area where I lived. It was the only countryside that I had encountered. We'd alight at 'The Jolly Roger' – a café that catered for the many boats moored in the area and passing strollers.

This picture shows a very frozen canal on a winter's day at Catforth.

Next to the stop on the way back there was always a pile of

milk churns awaiting collection. Upstairs on the bus the gangway was on the right with a selection of long benches, resembling church pews, stretching to the window on the left seating four or five passengers. The conductor had to reach over to collect fares and everyone on the row had to get up to let someone get off.

Another activity just before the end of the school summer holidays was to go blackberry picking. We still do this even now but are amazed by the children that are astounded by this eccentricity and interrogate us about what we are doing. After we had explained the predictable question would follow - Why?

On wet days board games were commonplace. We took it in turns to go to different houses to play. Everyone had a bike and that form of transport was used to get us to everywhere. On a glorious sunny day a cycle ride was an activity in it own right. Ad hoc ball games used to take place on every park and playing field. Many of these were adjacent to a railway line. All age groups used to play and stop whenever a train came. Even the youngest rail enthusiasts had substantial knowledge about their hobby being able to quote engine names and details of their allocations. It was quite educational the locomotive nameplates gave you knowledge of English cities, commonwealth countries, liners and even types of antelopes! We all wrote down the numbers in our notebooks and the games restarted. If there were just two or three we would take it in turns to shoot into a goal mouth, with jumpers substituting for the posts. A tree would serve as the stumps and a hedge as the wicket keeper for games of cricket.

Nowadays these areas are deserted. Only formal football matches seem to take place at the schools with children being driven to and from the game and parents complaining about the refereeing.

Playing fields like this on Cadley Causeway were well used by youngsters at weekends throughout the year and packed during evenings in spring and summer. The various ball games temporarily stopped whenever a train passed.

A great aid to train spotting at that time was the Ribble runabout ticket. This provided eight days consecutive travel from Saturday to Saturday on all routes served by buses operated by that company. Until you were 14 the ticket cost only 16 shillings. The services were extensive reaching

Liverpool and Manchester, Skipton in the east and included Barrow and Carlisle. For 10p a day this allowed us to visit all the engine sheds in the North West, go rambling in the Lake District and to the sea-side at Southport. The independence that was provided has vanished.

I have considerable sympathy for the lads that take an interest in such things as railways these days. They are often spurned by the others and given names such as 'nerds' or 'anoraks'. Their classmates apparently have far more constructive pastimes such as sitting on the wall in the rain next to the pub or pushing one another into the road by the Spar shop!

Many parks had an outdoor swimming pool only open in the summer months. It was 3d admittance to the one on Haslam Park. Around the pool were about forty changing cubicles where you placed your belongings. There were no locks – you just left everything on a little bench inside often next to those of someone else who you didn't know

The main swimming pool was in Saul Street in the town centre – an unwelcoming structure, dating back to the early 20th century, with two pools known as the small and large plunge. My memories of it consist of cold, draughty corridors some distance from the water itself. In the nineteen-seventies new swimming baths opened with much better, warm facilities in the new leisure centres. All the old pools closed, the Saul Street building being demolished to make way for the new law courts as shown below.

On a summer's afternoon at primary school, Haslam Park was a popular venue at which to have a science lesson. It was about quarter of an hour's walk from Roebuck Street Junior School. The whole class went with the teacher. Part of the journey was along the canal towpath where a slope led into the park. We'd identify the various plants and look for leaves and creatures such as caterpillars or tadpoles to take back to the nature table. After the formalities of the session were over, games of hide and seek would take place in the vicinity of this duck pond shown below and the search for trees that were easy to climb.

There was an inevitability that I was going to work in local government after having a temporary job there in 1970. That year I did not have work arranged for the summer when I returned home from university. A friend of my father who had a senior post in the Surveyor's Department of Lancashire County Council said that there was a job going for a couple of months if I wanted it. I took up the offer. As with the position at the supermarket there was no interview or meeting with anyone to see if you were suitable – it was simply yours if you wished to take it. The job consisted of working in an office with ten clerks, covering for holidays. Pay was £6-12-0 (£6.60) for a 37½-hour working week. At that time the wages were much lower than those which a permanent employee doing the same job would receive. The staff thought that if you were earning a £1000 a year in your early twenties that you were doing reasonably well. It is difficult to make a comparison with today's salaries because those jobs have disappeared.

It is perhaps worth reflecting on the prices of a few commonplace commodities then and now.

At most pubs a pint of bitter would cost just over 2 shillings or about 12p. With beer now costing more than £2 a pint this would be a nearly 20 fold rise.

A gigantic increase has been the charge to watch a football match. To stand behind the goal on Preston North End was 6/- or 30p, 35p to watch from the paddocks at the side. Most clubs, regardless of the division that they were in or how well they were doing, charged much the same. Recent entrance costs are well over £20 – with the benefit that you can sit down. This has risen more than 70 fold! The football programme that used to sell for 5p has become £2.

The bus fare to town was 6d (3p). This had risen to £1.20 or more. However recent improvements let you buy day or weekly tickets over the network that can make a great saving with free off-peak travel for pensioners.

Restrictive practices at the time prevented Preston Corporation transport from travelling outside the borough whilst a half empty Ribble bus could not pick up passengers waiting at a stop inside the boundary where the driver had just stopped to let someone alight.

A gallon of petrol at the time would be about 6/6d of 32p. We are all aware of the huge increases over the last two years. Astonishingly that would represent a rise of only about 16 times with more efficient engines enabling you to get many more miles to the gallon.

The office was located at the back of 9 Fishergate Hill in a wooden shed. In that office of ten, remarkably by today's standards all were men. The ages ranged from the office junior who was 17 and had left school the year before to people in their 40s and 50s. Only three owned a car and one a motor cycle. The only female staff in the building were two typists next door. Often at lunch time two wooden boxes were placed at each end of the room to be used as goals and the office became a football pitch with a tennis ball substituting for a football. After the match one player sitting in front of a fan to cool down was challenged when the boss came in.

'What's that fan on for Atherton?'

'Well I was feeling rather warm'

'Play less bloody football and do more work and you'll not feel so hot'.

Every day dozens of orders for equipment arrived in the office. These were predominantly in connection with road and pavement maintenance or street lighting. Each had a top sheet with three coloured copies beneath. Duties consisted of having a letter typed to an appropriate supplier of the materials that were needed and sending the top three copies with the letter. Details were checked word for word. The supplier retained one copy and passed the other two with the goods to the depot receiving them. The depot kept one and sent the signed copy back to the office. The invoices were then sent for payment. Orders, receipts and payments made seemed to be entered into ledgers and account books over and over again, with staff checking and double-checking each entry. Checkers checking the checkers! The forms were matched with signed copies and filed in order in folders. The temp had to catch up with much of the filing work that had been conveniently neglected during the year.

Some firms gave 2½% discount on bills that were paid promptly. These were rushed through and occasionally a photocopy was needed. Long before the days of each office having a desktop photocopier, the sheet to be copied had to be taken across the road to County Hall. There was just one photocopier in the whole building situated in a room operated by a lady in charge. You'd queue to wait for your copying being glared at all the time as though you were buying under age drink or a child skiving off school. The machine itself must have been over 6 feet in length having the features of a range cooker.

When I finished after eight weeks working there some of the permanent staff assured me 'I bet you don't want a job in local government.' 'Not flaming likely!'

It was only in the spring term in my final year at university that it occurred to me that I had to get a job that summer – a real job for life – a career! Until then it was not something that I had ever considered. Work was something that you did in the holidays! You took your O levels. Most people left then at 16. Five O level passes was quite enough to get you into banking or a building society (with a very attractive mortgage rate). It would get you into administration in the private sector, the NHS, Civil Service, local government or most other occupations. In fact 5 O levels had much the same buying power as a degree today - without the student loan! If you then went on pass two or three A levels that would enable you to become an accountant or management trainee.

There was no such thing as careers advice at the grammar school in those days. The nearest thing was a teacher telling us in the sixth form 'You get a good degree in physics or maths and the world's your oyster.' Only a minority of us then went on to university at that time. It was like an extension of the grammar school. You studied say geography or English at A level then you continued with the same subject at university because you liked it and you were good at it. You had no thoughts as to where it may lead you in the future. Subjects such as business, media and leisure studies were unheard of. Only students studying engineering, law or medicine had some notion about what they actually wanted to do.

Another huge change that has occurred over the years is students having part-time jobs. Nowadays almost all youths aged 15 upwards seem to have weekend and evening jobs at the retail parks, restaurants and serving food in pubs. In fact the part-time work that you have done is sometimes regarded by employers as more relevant than your qualifications. Apart from paper rounds or helping with milk deliveries it was almost totally unknown during term time forty years ago.

After graduating I was unemployed. It was a case of looking through the Lancashire Evening Post and the university lists of vacancies suitable for someone with a maths degree. These tended to be in accounts, computing and areas such as (O&M) Organisation and Method – not one designed to make you the most popular person if looking for efficiency and staff savings. As today the accent was on people with experience. I had one interview at a major employer in the Preston area. The interviewer's first statement (not likely to go down very well these days) was 'I hope you're better than that drip that I've just interviewed'. 'Probably not' I replied. I wasn't taken on.

Later in the summer I did get an appointment as a trainee programmer at an insurance company. I have to admit that when I started work I hadn't the faintest idea about what programming in a commercial environment was or what a systems analyst did. I though it might be like university where you wrote programs to do calculations and statistics not to print insurance policies. Unfortunately that job was in Liverpool. After looking for accommodation and finding that most were located some miles out I decided to live with my parents and travel from home each day. The poor public transport and waste of time and money commuting that prevented you from undertaking such activities as attending night school classes made me determined that I would look for a job nearer home when the opportunity arose and ensure that I never had to travel again.

The following year I successfully applied for a post at Preston Polytechnic (as it had just become and long before obtaining university status). Just two of us were interviewed as one person had dropped out. It was remarkable how once you had attained some expertise and experience that getting jobs was quite easy. Here I wrote computer programs in COBOL, FORTRAN and PLAN languages on a very old fashioned ICL 1901 machine. It had only 64k of memory. The computer here was put to a very limited use with minimal administrative needs and mostly used for coursework and lecturers' research projects in engineering topics.

Quite incredibly when compared to today, when it was

switched on in the morning it had to be loaded with a big wheel of paper tape. Computer files were all secured to this medium and input data for students, lecturers and administrative uses was punched onto cards.

The work that I did was interesting enough, including taking part in experiments. There was the opportunity to carry out research to obtain a PhD and plenty of scope to participate in sporting activities – badminton or 5 a side football – some of it taking place during the working day!

Unfortunately at that time I did not have sufficient work to occupy me and was too junior to know how to go looking for it and applied to a couple of other firms. In 1974 I was appointed to the Data Processing Division within the Treasurers Department of Lancashire County Council located at County Hall.

## 2

## THE NINETEEN SEVENTIES

The letters of appointment in those days resembled something from forty years earlier.

Dear Kitchen

You have been appointed as a junior systems analyst on a starting salary of £1926 commencing on 20 May 1974.

Signed by the County Treasurer.

Everyone received equally polite letters – Dear Smith or Dear Roberts, as though you were still at the Grammar School, although presumably female staff did receive a Dear Miss Jones. There was nothing so courteous as I am pleased to tell you or I look forward to meeting you.

This went on for a number of years until one person leaving his post sent his letter of resignation to the Treasurer in the form

Dear Cunliffe

I shall be terminating my employment with you with effect from June 17th.

Yours sincerely

John Bromley

The head of the Data Processing Division was called in to account for his staff's demeanour – 'was this some silly prank?' 'Obviously he thought it was the protocol Mr. Cunliffe'

From then on it was Dear Mr. Bromley!

Nowadays with the accent on customer care, staff welfare, accreditation, investment in people and motivation it is hard to credit the 'Old School Tie' syndrome that was still prevalent in the early seventies. The culture was much more 'Find somebody to blame!' 'Heads will roll' was heard. One young employee walking along was told by a senior officer, acting as a sergeant major from the nineteen fifties 'Get your haircut laddie'. The whole council seemed to hanker to the military with words like 'staff mess' rather than 'canteen' or 'refectory' and 'leave' or 'absent' instead of 'on holiday' or 'sick'. There was such a lack of trust that letters had to be signed by no lower than an assistant treasurer before they could be put in the post.

A lady who liked to bounce along the corridor was given an ultimatum 'Either you put on a bra or you wear a cardigan!' On another occasion the diktat went out 'Anyone leaving unwashed milk bottles outside the door will be sacked!'

Sexism was rife. A maxim of a member of the personnel team was 'Two at eye level is better than four at O-level!' A popular pastime was to pinch female's bottoms. I was often quite a shock to some men when a couple of women issued similar treatment! In today's world when the norm is to live with a partner rather than or before getting married, forty years ago a relationship was regarded as such a scandal that one woman openly living with her boy friend (still married to someone else) was told as a minimum to change her name.

Some questions asked of women at interviews are unimaginable compared to today. 'What happens if you get married and leave?' or 'When do you intend to start a family?' for instance. Some were told that they could not be considered for a post because there were no ladies toilets!

At the time when I started my employment local government in general and Lancashire in particular had just undergone major reorganisation.

Until then Lancashire consisted of (I believe) 17 boroughs. These were the main towns such as Manchester, Liverpool, Wigan, Bolton and Barrow in Furness out on a limb. Only four previously independent boroughs (Blackpool, Preston, Blackburn and Burnley) were to be part of the new County of Lancashire.

Those old authorities used to handle all services in their local areas form street lighting to staffing schools and even issuing their own car registrations.

The new Lancashire was much smaller than its predecessor, great chunks being absorbed into Cheshire, Merseyside, Greater Manchester and a new county of Cumbria. The County Council was responsible for services like Education, Social Services, Highways and Libraries. There were 14 new District Councils created. These districts dealt with such things as council housing and refuse collection and sent out the rates and ballot cards for themselves and on behalf of Lancashire County Council.

Four of them corresponded to the previous boroughs increased in size whilst there were new ones created such as West Lancashire, Hyndburn and Rossendale.

As well as reorganisation it was also a time of great expansion in local government. In lots of cases these new councils required experienced staff particularly in the field of computers. Many vacancies were filled from Lancashire. Three out of seven senior analysts obtained jobs in this way and resigned at the same time. This provided early promotions for some young staff within the council.

Those early days of computing were as far removed from today as the Middle Ages.

Abbreviations such as IT or ICT were unknown. An 'IT Person'? More likely an 'It Girl' – an attractive young lady just starting to make an impact in the cinema. Opening windows was something that you did with a latch and spreadsheets the work of chambermaids! A CD would be the 'Corps Diplomatique.' As for a mouse on your desk!

A hard disk was very much that. A heavy cylinder like piece of apparatus that could be exchanged for another to be bolted on to a disk drive machine. It would hold 8 megabytes of storage. 8 million characters, considered enormous at the time, probably costing hundreds of pounds. Today a memory card for your camera may hold a gigabyte or 1000 million characters and would be the size of your fingernail. It might cost you less than £10 and that could include 50 free photographs printed from it!

Up to this time computer staff had normally been taken from existing employees from a variety of sections. Some had been appointed from a section dealing with foster parents another from wages.

An advertisement would appear in the internal bulletin inviting staff who were interested in becoming programmers to attend an informal interview with the section head and sit an aptitude test. Suitable candidates were taken on. This was an excellent method of filling posts. There were no expensive adverts to place, interview arrangements or travel to pay and the persons appointed had already proven themselves in their previous position. The aptitude test was a fair way of determining that someone was up to the logic skills that were needed. A vacancy would then be created at the most junior level for a school leaver.

The Data Processing Division was divided into five sections - Systems Analysts, Programmers, Computer Operators, Clerks and Punch room staff.

The job of the systems analyst was to investigate what various parts of the council did and determine the feasibility of computerising some of the work. Most early systems were financial such as paying salaries or creditors. One in which I had early involvement was the paying of student grants and fees. A colleague was occupied with bringing in computers into the Police Force. An Inspector introduced him to the Administrative Section with the words 'This is the man who is going to make you all redundant!'

In most sections there was comparatively little scope for computerisation. There were no screens at this time. All data was entered onto specifically designed forms. The information was all keyed in by staff in the punch room. Initially it was exactly that, holes punched into cards or paper tape. Later it was entered directly onto magnetic tapes knows as Mohawks.

This must have been a very soul destroying job. At least the typists could make sense of what they were typing but in the punch room it was a collection of meaningless letters and numbers. The information entered by the first clerk was then verified by a second to find any mistakes. There were surprisingly few. To attain a pay rise the staff had to reach 8000, 10000 and 12000 key depressions per hour with a small error rate.

At that time the punch room consisted of 40 daytime staff with an additional evening shift. We used to comment that whatever else happened in the world of computing there would always be a need for punch room staff. How wrong we were!

After accepting that computerisation of part of the work of a section was feasible in terms of cost, staff or time saving and other efficiencies, the systems analysts wrote *program specifications*. This broke down the work into various functions. More often than not these would consist of something like - Validation of the data that had been entered onto tape, Maintain a Name and Address file, Update a Master File of transactions and various procedures to make payments or send out bills that may be run daily or monthly and Month End or Year End jobs that would archive information that had been completed. Other aspects would provide statistical summaries or allow enquiries to be made. This was many years before databases and query languages.

Programmers translated these specifications into program code. They were written onto sometimes dozens of coding sheets. Pencils had to be used so that errors could easily be erased and corrections made. This did encourage care. When complete these sheets also went to the punch room.

Until the early 1970s the programming language used was known as PLAN. This was a very early, first generation, programming language where even the smallest task required a series of instructions. From that time all new applications were written in COBOL, which had become universal. The old PLAN systems were being rewritten in this language. FORTRAN was also used but only for some applications of a scientific nature in the Planning and Surveyors departments.

In today's world when you just create a document or other file without any thought of where it is stored or how large, it is hard to believe the effort that it once was.

Each hard disk was mapped into *cylinders*. If you were creating a file containing for example customer's names and addresses you had to calculate the expected number of records and file size and carefully plan the layout, saving a character on each record if you could. A program called

XPJC was then run to allocate the space onto the hard disk, preventing anyone else from using that area.

Another program XPJJ was used to see what had been allocated and how much of that allocation had actually been used.

When your programming sheets had been entered onto tape it was submitted to the computer room for compilation or translation into code that the machine could understand. XPLM compiled PLAN programs and XEKB those written in COBOL.

Coding had to be checked and double-checked. You could usually only submit two runs a day. If there were any coding errors the program would not compile. They had to be corrected and resubmitted. An error might be for instance entering the word PERFOM instead of PERFORM. This was before the program was tested for mistakes in its logic.

A machine was available where you could punch individual cards yourself to make corrections.

Some programming staff used to feel that the systems analysts regarded themselves as more important than the rest of the workforce. One remarked to the chief systems analyst that half the systems analysts were wankers. 'You can't go round saying that'. 'Very well, I'll take it back. Half the systems analysts are not wankers!'

In those days there were two shifts of computer operators who had to store and bring disks from the storeroom and load magnetic tapes from the many racks. All computer stationery consisted of continuous sheets, pre-printed payslips or invoices for instance or green and white for most reports and program listings. Today these are completely unknown but for years offices were awash with them.

There was a reception area where staff from different sections brought jobs to be run on the computer – not merely from within County Hall but from various other buildings from around the town. An office of clerks had to sort out jobs that these different sections had submitted. An example might be to bring a batch of invoices to pay, to validate them, update the creditors payments file and print cheques. The data was submitted to the Punch Room. A card would be punched that would accompany the tape produced in Punch. The card might say run job CRED2 that would run a series of programs. When complete a validation report, the cheques and the original data would be packaged together for the section to collect. Normally the system would work without any hiccups but it occasionally failed and the analyst and programmer involved in the system would sort out the problem. Tapes used for security back up were recorded and stored in safes.

These general methods of working carried on for as much as another ten years. Nobody could believe that there was any other way of working and that it would always be like that.

At that time local government and the civil service did not have much of a reputation for very hard work. It was regarded by many as a job for life. Nothing very glamorous or spectacular but a steady income. The highlights of the day were lunchtime and tea breaks.

Once I was asked where I worked. I said 'County Hall'. 'Oh you mean the home of rest!' was his reply.

From then on I played along with them. 'Whereabouts do you work?' 'Oh, I don't work I'm in local government!' One colleague on a course was asked 'How many people work in County Hall?' 'Less than half' was her instant response and the county council mottos jokingly became 'Never do today what you can leave until tomorrow' and 'Why do a job with one person when you could use two?'

One major change that came in during the mid 1970s, as it did in most offices, was the introduction of flexi-time. Until then office hours had been 8.45 am to 5 pm. At the end of the day it was a mass walk out resembling the buzzer going in a factory.

Flexi-time was a great bonus to the staff. People that wanted to start early and avoid the traffic could do so without having to waste half an hour arriving early and reading the newspaper. Those that preferred to set off late could leave at 6pm when the roads were quieter. This gave office coverage for longer hours. It especially suited staff who came on the train and previously could not catch one that left at say 16.55.

Management gained a great deal. Before flexi-time many staff would have lunch in the canteen and then go shopping in the town centre. An hour had been allotted for lunch but there was no accountability in the days prior to the clock cards that accompanied flexi-time. With flexi-working most staff only took half an hour for lunch but could take an hour or two if they needed to go home or shopping. The original clock cards were not very sophisticated. A machine merely printed your clocking in and clocking out times. You had to add up the hours worked each day yourself. Lunch times had to be a minimum of half an hour, any time before 8.00am or after 6.15 pm did not count. You had to work out the hours worked each day and subtract 36 hours 15 minutes. You were not allowed to have more than 2 hours debit or 3 hours 15 minutes credit at the end of each four week period. It was a few years later before we were allowed to take leave for flexi-time that had been built up.

Whilst the four boroughs that had existed prior to 1974 had their own staff with expertise in writing computer systems the new districts did not. Many subscribed to systems that Lancashire ran on their behalves. These included the Payroll, Accounting, Loans and Creditor Payments systems that also ran here but in addition Rates, Rents, Housing Advances and Register of Electors systems that did not.

Extra computer staff (paid for by those district councils) were taken on to handle this work. A Computer Liaison Officer was employed at each district who was responsible for managing the systems. In some cases systems that ran in other councils were used instead of writing them ourselves from scratch. In those days they were often provided free of charge.

This was sometimes false economy. Staff here had to understand their programs (in which they had had no involvement). Those imported to handle the Rates had so many little individual programs that you had to amend a dozen or so to make minor changes to the system.

Another was brought in from elsewhere to give loans for properties that Building Societies would not provide. This involved calculating the monthly repayment amounts – a straightforward formula. Unfortunately the people that had written the system were unaware of the formula and instead had tables of each amount, period and interest rate that filled up an entire disk!

Each district sent its data on hand-written forms here to be entered onto the Mohawk tapes along with everything else. The only difference was that the jobs were then initiated remotely from those district offices. There were no screens in those days. There was a couple of consoles in the machine room and at the district councils that clattered away printing job status information like the football scores on the BBC teleprinter or your list of purchases at Tesco.

At this time canteen amenities were quite limited. There was a small restaurant in the main building but also an informal club facility in a house on Bow Lane from which you could get a drink, watch television, and have a game of snooker or a pie and peas.

Cooking facilities were somewhat primitive in those days. Words like hygiene were not part of every day vocabulary. Staff used to smoke whilst serving dinner. One day some ash off the end of her cigarette fell into the gravy. No problem though – just stir it in. After all the most suitable way to discover whether the fat was hot enough in the local chip shop was to spit into it!

This was replaced by an excellent facility on the top floor of a new building that opened soon after.

The nineteen-seventies was a time of great opportunity. All businesses were expanding their use of computers. They were all mainframe machines located in a very specific 'computer room' where the temperature had to maintained at very precise levels.

It reminds me of an occasion when a manager was contacting other councils concerning their methods of controlling the temperature.

'Could I speak with your Data Processing Manager?' After a pause, 'Well your computer manager then'. A further pause – 'The person that looks after your computer room'.

Yet another. 'Someone who is responsible for the purchase of computer hardware or consumables'. This time there was a much longer delay followed by 'Well if you did have a computer!'

For people willing to move around there was an abundance of jobs advertised in the computer magazines – in management, team leaders and programmer/analysts at all levels, especially for those willing to work in the south east. Almost all programming was in COBOL. Systems work was similar regardless of the business. For those of us wishing to stay there were also opportunities here as others left. There was plenty of highly paid contract work for varying lengths of time.

Some people took the opportunity of temporary or permanent jobs abroad. Two-year contracts in the Middle East with an optional third year were popular. The salary of a fairly senior analyst would be about £5000 in the mid to late seventies. Tax-free salaries of over £20000 and free accommodation were being offered. That would be about £150,000 today. Three staff went independently to work on contracts in Kuwait. One chap who went out found a job for his wife teaching English on about £70,000 at today's prices. It was joked that his kids were doing paper rounds equivalent to about £500 a week! One of the main problems was what you did on you return. It would be somewhat of a let down to come back to the sort of job that you had left.

One member of staff emigrated to Australia. He wrote us a

letter telling us that Australians did not believe that the British get washed and sent us some Pommie jokes bearing this in mind.

Where does a Pommie hide his wallet?   -   Underneath the soap.
How many Pommies can you get into a shower 10ft by 8 ft? - None.
What does a Pommie do with a dirty shirt? – Wear it.
How often does a Pommie change his socks? – Once a month, regardless of whether they're dirty!

We could always retaliate with jokes about Australians' foreplay.

'Are you up for it Sheila?' or alternatively 'Are y'awake?'

This reminds me of the experience of some colleagues travelling abroad.

One friend was visiting Moscow for a few days. A member of his party had a large beard, resembling Brian Blessed and looking very suspicious.

The man behind the desk checking his passport asked, in the voice of a James Bond villain 'Are you a terrorist?' Unfortunately the poor chap thought that he said 'tourist' and replied 'Yes!' Security officers instantly took him away. He must have thought that he was well on the way to Siberia until the misunderstanding was resolved.

Another from the office had travelled with a friend to Morocco. On the journey to the hotel the cab driver asked them 'Sprechen Sie Deutsch?' No, we're English they replied. 'Parlez-vous français?' 'No no we're English, English'. 'Do you not have schools in England?'

They retreated from the taxi feeling about three feet tall!

A further person was waiting for the lift in a New York hotel. As she entered three 'heavies' got in, a terrifying sight making her want to alight as soon as she could. When the door was closing one shouted 'Hit the floor!' She instantly crouched down on her hands and knees terrified that somebody was about to pull out a gun. You can imagine her embarrassment when she realised that all he meant was for her to press the button for the basement!

The only similar incident that I can remember from my own experience was at a youth hostel where an American girl was baffled by the miniature packets of cereal known as 'Kellogs Variety' and in desperation asked 'Will somebody tell me how the hell I cook these damn things?'

Apart from staff very little changed over the next few years. Because computers had only been around for less than ten years almost everyone was in their twenties and thirties. There were few retirements in the division. Most women who became pregnant resigned their posts and stayed at home for a few years.

In the mid seventies the original 1900 series computer was replaced by a 2900 series. This ran alongside the earlier machine for a number of years. Systems running on the old machine had (if they were suitable) to be converted to run on the new one. The new computer could not run applications written in PLAN so these had to be completely rewritten from scratch. This was probably the last time that huge, individual, tailor made payroll and accounting systems were written anywhere.

As planning the changes was an enormous job, a new senior analyst post was created to handle the work. It was envisaged that one of the most experienced senior staff would wish to take on the work. However none was keen as a lot of unpaid overtime was involved so an external applicant was appointed. People coming from outside firms were more accustomed to making their own decisions rather than having to pass them up the line and were often frustrated as the consequent delays. This officer was reportedly on a motoring holiday with his wife and family in France. On the day he was due to return to work a message was received from Canada saying that he'd taken employment there and wasn't returning to Britain!

It was much easier to create and handle computer files on this new machine but apart from that computing carried on as before. The computer was still an enormous device, stacked away in a designated room. Operators managed the day to day running and only specialised programmers could actually store their own files and programs. It was all regarded as very esoteric by non-computer staff.

At this time security cards to gain entry to the computer room were brought in for the first time. Until then there was no security in the building. You could just walk in and out of the machine room. Only a handful of staff had a card and managers struggled to gain access. However on one occasion the milkman was found wandering about the room looking for his money for the week having attained access with no difficulty!

For the first time Visual Display Units became available. A few sections such as salaries had one so that staff could determine if pay runs had been done, check addresses or salary details. VDUs replaced the old consoles in the computer room and a few were available in a corner of the programmers' room. This was a great bonus enabling us to make alterations without punching cards or sending coding sheets to the punch room. It was still a long way from having a screen on your desk.

Regularly the system broke down or crashed as it became known. A most meaningful message appeared on the screen – 'Hardware or software error detected!'

Occasionally a visitor from a college would arrive to see what a computer room looked like and what programmers did. They were shown an early 'Golf Game.' Here the computer would display on the screen 'you are 410 yards from the hole. What club do you require?' You might enter a driver. It would now say that you are 150 yards from the hole and which club would you require? You'd say a 7 iron for example and finally a putter and the computer would inform you that you had holed in 4. You tend to cringe at the thought today with machines that have graphics showing perfect pictures of the world's courses as though you're actually at the open, sound effects and controls that let you strike the ball like Tiger Woods. Thirty years ago that was all that was on offer.

Each VDU in the building had a number stuck above the screen. The screens in the programmers' office may be VD16 and VD19. The letters fell off from the machine where a lady was working fell off and she proclaimed 'I've lost my VD!' That was the start of 'the book of innuendos.' This was soon followed by another entry, talking about swimming in the sea. 'I like in on top, my boy friend prefers it underneath!'

Life went on with little change. Each systems analyst and programming team was responsible for a miss-match of applications. A few of us became Programmer/Analysts long before this becoming the standard. New projects were issued to those people that did not have too heavy a work load at the time. Many of them involved rewriting systems that had been written in PLAN into systems written in COBOL. Improvements that had been requested by the users were incorporated into the revised systems. Two examples that I was given to convert dealt with the payment and receipt of income from those staff entitled to a Car

Loan and the Register of Shot Guns that ran at Police HQ.

At the end of the decade Lancashire became responsible for the publication of the 'Police Accounting Statistics.' Information was collected from each of the 44 police forces. Programs were written to handle and collate the data and to produce a booklet to provide tabulations and compare aspects of each force.

Most computer output at the time was printed on the green and white continuous manuscript paper. It was all in capital letters with only numerals and punctuation such as full stops and commas. The output from this system was on plain white continuous paper. That was far from commonplace. Because the booklet had headings that required printing in lower case letters meant that the computer operators had actually to change the print barrel whenever a print run was activated.

I was given this project that only ten years later would have been barely a couple of days work for somebody with data being entered into spreadsheets. These would easily validate the input and from them charts and graphs could be readily produced. With the software available at the time the task took over two months.

# 3

# THE EARLY NINETEEN EIGTHIES

One fantastic thing about County Hall was its location. At this time the great majority of people lived in the Preston area. Buses from Leyland, Penwortham and Ashton stopped almost outside the building. There was ample car parking. Cycle stands were provided in the basement. The railway station was a few minutes walk away. This was ideal for people travelling to meetings in London and Manchester who could park in the early morning at County Hall and stroll across to catch their train

There was plenty to do at lunch times. There was a bowling green only a few minutes walk down Fishergate Hill and a sports centre at Penwortham Holme, with two tennis courts and an all weather pitch. It was simple to recruit ten people to play five a side football. Other staff played in a squash ladder. With flexi time it was easy to fit in a drive to the leisure centre, a game and shower in an hour and a half.

The library was just over a ten minute walk. Most people went to the shops in the town centre. It was surprising what you could buy in half an hour. Nearby was a bookshop called 'Sweetens'. For years this was the number one shop of its kind in the area. An additional business developed at the shop writing software for suppliers and retailers of books. Several programming staff were poached from the council.

Sweetens was the last shop in the area to still close for

Wakes Week even in the nineteen-eighties

As would be expected there were plenty of pubs and cafes in the vicinity. Avenham Park was less than a ten-minute walk away providing a stroll along the river. At the edge of the park was an excellent pub 'The Continental'. It was exactly that, serving meals and drinks outside, something that was not common in those days. It had a first class children's playground.

Certain officers had some unusual methods of passing their dinnertimes. One lady rather than wash dishes in the sink in the kitchen area preferred to wash her hair in it most days and would then put her head down for a quick kip on the draining board! Another used to clear all the files off her desk and cut out her sewing patterns. She did tell me that had she been able to carry it, she'd have brought her sewing machine to work.

It was this 'well-being' that helped to keep many of us at the county, rather than looking for more lucrative jobs elsewhere that would not have had these attractions.

One change that occurred following the conservatives winning the general election in 1979 was the start of 'Competitive Tendering.' Until this time the council employed its own staff to provide school meals, maintain playing fields and grounds at police stations for example. The first group of staff to be put out to competition were those who maintained the roads and footpaths.

At this time a company had an affiliation with the firm who supplied the computer, any upgrades and dealt with any hardware problems that the operators could not sort out. These were mostly IBM or ICL computers. We were told that we were an ICL Authority. The same company also wrote the software to deal with the competition that had been imposed on the Surveyors Department. I felt that the system had been put together in a rush. We had to test all the programs and report the errors that we found and put together the control language that would actually run those that were required. The system was known as DILIS (Standing for something like Direct Labour Information System). It was a coincidence that the wife of one main user of the system was called Dilys. This was the precursor of software having acronyms. Before then it was the 'Payroll' or 'Libraries Purchasing System'. Programs just had numbers such as PA05.

Until this time if a job was needed such as a road requiring resurfacing it was done by the council's own staff. From this time each task went out to tender. The council's own labour force could bid for the work but the entire costs of the job had to be built in. This included the wages, materials and administrative charges. In addition the system had to demonstrate that the work force was fully occupied, earning their keep from such jobs and having no gaps when they had no work. If there were then the work force had to be cut. This was a very effective way of making the council look for new methods of working to reduce costs and make the business much more efficient in order to compete with private firms. By imposing these efficiencies ensured that the Council labour force did win most contracts.

In the eighties came an invention that only a few years before nobody would have believed the impact - the introduction of word processors and microcomputers. Like the discovery of electricity in the nineteenth century, regarded as a source of amusement rather than having any practical applications, at that time micros were thought of as having limited use. One devotee at a meeting talking about the 'unlimited future of micros' was overruled by the DP manager who asserted that 'No! His mainframe computer was limitless.' I think that the question today is more likely to be 'What is a mainframe computer? - Something in a museum.'

Until this time typists used to merely type memos, letters and reports from hand-written copies. Some managers could reel off a letter verbally and a secretary would copy it down in short hand to type up later. To underline something you had to first type it and then go back to the start of the word and press the underline key several times. An improvement had been the introduction of a memory typewriter. These had a small screen where you would enter a line, correct it if necessary, and then print it. Even this was quite an advance when compared to the many letters that you used to read with words crossed out with 'x's.

The first word processors obtained for the type rooms were 8800 machines. As we were an ICL Authority needless to say these were manufactured by ICL. The fact that you could store several pages without printing it or insert a paragraph that someone wanted as an afterthought was a godsend. It was a fantastic step forward even though it was a dedicated machine that could do nothing else. As I sit typing this using MS Word, I find it incredible that in the past authors must have had a mental picture beforehand of everything that they wanted to say.

It did create its own problems. A teacher had his CV held as a file on a word processor. He had applied for a senior post at a school say Barden. He was unsuccessful with that application and on a later occasion he had modified it when applying for a position at another school such as Towneley. He provided details of his achievements and some of the contributions that he could make at Towneley school. However he omitted to change the last line which stated '… and that it why I am keen to apply for this vacancy at Barden school.'

Coinciding with the word processors was the introduction of microcomputers. The first departments to obtain them were the Architects and Police HQ. Each of these had dedicated staff developing applications. For the first time, instead of requesting work to go on the development schedule in Treasurers Department, staff in these areas could simply sit at the computer and get on with the work. Suddenly the computer was no longer a huge beast locked away in a cage somewhere but had become akin to a family pet that could sit it an ordinary office.

The Education Department not wanting to miss out also bought one at the beginning of 1983. These micros were known as DRS 20 series machines. Of course like everything else they were provided by ICL. This machine costing about £6000 was cheap in comparison to the mainframe computer but astronomic compared to today's computers. The entire disk space available was about 20 megabytes. It was quite an original concept. You could link a dozen or so satellite computers to the DRS 20/50 than ran programs stored on that hub.

Unlike the other departments that had specific plans for their new equipment, at that time the Education Department had none. Somehow management felt that it would 'simply do something on its own!' For the best part of a year it just sat there.

Later in 1983 a new post was created of 'Computer Development Officer' to make the machine work. I applied for the job, was appointed that year and started employment within the Education Department where I have been since.

You had to be very careful deciding what was suitable for these new micros. One department held some manual records on forms in a cabinet. They decided to computerise them using their newly acquired DRS micro. However after loading the records onto the computer they asked the question 'What have we actually achieved?' Information could be retrieved from the computer of course but that was no different from going directly to the physical files.

On my last day in the Treasurers Department I took part in a party trick that if I hadn't actually been a participant I wouldn't have believed it possible.

You sit on a chair. Four people stand round it in a square. Each one puts their index and middle fingers of each hand under the edge of the chair and attempts to lift it with me or other gullible person sat on it. Needless to say it scarcely moves.

Each person in turn takes their right hand fingers from under the chair and places them onto the sitter's head. They then do that with the other hand. They to the reverse, restoring the fingers under the chair. Next a further attempt is made to raise the seat and hey presto – the chair plus 12 stone is lifted 4 feet into the air. We repeated the process with someone substantially heavier!

On joining the Education Department I found that computer equipment in the entire service consisted of one DRS 20 series 50 machine and a printer and a couple of VDUs. Programs could be written for the DRS 20 and it could also be connected to the mainframe computer as a terminal. You could easily display and accept information from the screen. If the values that had been entered were invalid or inconsistent an appropriate message was sent to the screen asking for it to be corrected. This was a great stride from batches of forms being sent to the punch room and then run on the mainframe computer with erroneous records having to be resubmitted.

Characters on the screen were all the same size. 80 could be displayed across the screen and there was room for just 25 rows. There was no such thing as a screen saver. If it was left on for long periods of time the contents were etched into it. This early microprocessor did not even have the date or time built into it. Staff at that time were unaccustomed to having a computer upon their desk tops. Pipe tobacco, crumbs of cheese and orange juice were amongst the things spilt into the keyboard.

The printer was prehistoric compared to today. A line at a time was printed. Ribbons were wound round spools in exactly the same way as those on a typewriter. Every letter and number occupied the same space. There were no italics or bolding. At least upper and lower case characters could both be printed!

At that time there was very little computer usage within the Education Department. Apart from staff on the Payroll system (teachers, school cleaners, college lecturers along with police, fire officers and social services employees) and statistics about the workforce the two systems running on the mainframe computer, specifically for the Education Department, were the paying of Students Grants and fees and Further Education Students Records (FESR) where a record was maintained for everyone attending any courses in the local colleges or night school class. This was effectively a mass of data entered over a short period of time with boxes of tens of thousands of forms piled up on top of each other. Reports were provided that showed numbers of pupils enrolled for each type of course, subject and establishment from which funding was determined. To extract further information from the application necessitated using an ICL query product known as FILETAB. This was quite an ingenious product for the time in which you coded 'decision tables.'

Initially the application that dealt with student grants originated in Leeds. We were provided with all their programs with the coding and then we converted them to meet the requirements for Lancashire. It was known as the FE Awards system although they were grants for Higher rather than Further Education. As with other systems at this time the student who had received a place at a university or other establishment completed an application form that provided details of their course and parental income from which the grant would be determined. Clerks in the section copied relevant data onto computer input forms. There was a set of forms to provide for changes to addresses or other circumstances. The data was submitted to the reception desk in the Data Processing Section for entry into the punch room and then a job created to be run by computer operators. Finally a large package was available for collection.

This would consist of the original input forms, validation report and documents for the student showing the amount of grant that they would receive along with the parental contribution. Only one batch of data could be submitted each week so that any input error had to be corrected for the following week's run. Provided that the application was sent in good time this was seldom a problem.

Just before the start of each term a payment run was submitted that would produce a cheque for each student sent to the bursar at the establishment.

This was quite different to today's situation of student loans. There was a minimum grant of £50 even if you were a millionaire. Everyone had fees paid on their behalf unless their parents had refused to declare their income. Students even received an amount for excess travel – this could be quite substantial for someone attending a university such as Southampton. If you had to stay for some extra weeks over the normal 30 you also received additional money for those.

Personally I feel that university life was much easier in those days. Most of us had accommodation in the halls of residence, with meals cooked for us, bedding changed, TV lounges and sporting activities available on site without needing to step outside the building. The university lecture theatres were only a half hour walk away. The normal grant was about £430 per year when I was in my final year. Most parents made up the difference between the amount that you received, assessed on their income and that £430. Hall fees came to about £70 for each term, leaving you with about £4 a week plus whatever you earned during your summer vacation. Nowadays people graduate having accrued five figure debts. Owing money was virtually unheard of in those days. The worst that could happen was to be overdrawn in you account by say £40.

Many local students came to the enquiry desk to ask about their grants particularly if there had been a delay. Whilst most were very polite some were aggressive and resorted to shouting or swearing at staff in the section who were only trying to do their job. One employee being treated in his manner had had enough and told the student. 'Look we may be a convenience to the public but we are not here to be shit upon!' This became an often quoted story throughout the department.

On another occasion there had been some form of industrial action leading to delays to students receiving their grants. To avoid large numbers of students coming to the enquiry desk a sign saying 'School Buildings Section' had replaced that saying student grants. However some wag had written underneath it 'and secret passage to student grants!'

At this time the Education Department ran a Careers Service. Each town within the county had a careers office from which staff went into the local high schools to give advice on jobs, training schemes and opportunities for further education.

The intention was to computerise the entire business. There would be no completion of forms. It was all to be screen based giving remote access to a system originally developed by Berkshire council that was held on our mainframe computer. These small offices had screens (dumb terminals as they became known) that were merely linked to the mainframe, the careers section in County Hall used a DRS 20 model 10 that was linked via the DRS 20 model 50.

Information regarding pupils' interests and aspirations were entered on the screen and a print-out was produced detailing careers and training that met these requirements. Some of us entered data to see what the system would come up with for us. It produced quite a variety but none suggested working with computers or in local government! For me it suggested an agricultural economist but I didn't see many jobs of that nature advertised in the vacancy columns of the local newspaper even if I knew what one was!

At this time it was decided that there should be more staff expertise in matters of health and safety. Some officers attended fire awareness training and each corridor had a fire warden. If there was a fire drill these people were responsible for ensuring that there was nobody left in the offices and that everyone was accounted for. This was when IRA activity was at its worst. There had been several attacks on the mainland. It was inescapable that there would be telephone calls stating that there was a bomb in the building. County Hall was evacuated regularly. The same applied to other office blocks and shopping centres everywhere. The great majority were hoaxes but nothing could be taken for granted. Sometimes when we had left the building a message would be announced over the load speaker telling us that information had been received that there was a bomb in the building. Volunteers were required to look for it! Some people actually did! Ten minutes later another announcement would tell us that the whole building had been searched and it was safe to return to our desks. Such reassurance!

For many years a nurse had been employed in County Hall. She would soon be finishing so some of us had attended First Aid training. Much was aimed at the different methods of artificial respiration including mouth to mouth known as the kiss of life, putting a person in the recovery position and placing bandages to secure broken arms until the medical service arrived. After several sessions each person that had been to the training had a test.

One was asked what is the usual name for mouth to mouth resuscitation. The kiss of death she replied! However that was a very apt description for the solution of another person being examined. If someone's heart had stopped you were to attempt to revive it by striking the sternum or breast bone. When asked how she would restart the heart the candidate said 'I'd apply a sharp blow to the scrotum!'

I don't believe that the nurse had been over occupied but only a few days after she retired an officer collapsed into a diabetic coma. We telephoned for an ambulance and tried to pour some sweet tea into her lips before it arrived as we had been trained, very much concerned that we may be making matters worse.

First aid training did prove essential to a colleague who dragged someone from the sea whilst on holiday. His quick response and mouth to mouth resuscitation saved the patient's life and he received an award for his action.

Most areas of the Education Department where there was scope for using computers were small scale developments that could be written fairly quickly and easily using this new microcomputer. There was no need to involve the mainframe computer or Data Processing Services. Some examples were School meals, assessment tests done by the Psychological Service (long before SATS) and holding details of schools governing bodies. Unlike the mainframe computer where data was backed up to magnetic tapes, floppy disks were used here. These really were floppy disks. Seven inch circular entities, like vinyl records, that could be bent. They could store about 360,000 characters of information. In future disk drives would be identified by letters such as A: and C: On these machines they were known as £0 or £1.

One use made by the Catering Service was to cost recipes and menus used in school meals, based on the prices of ingredients at the time. Again this was before the days of spreadsheets simplifying the process. Another purpose was to determine their nutritional value in terms of vitamins, carbohydrates and level of fat. The local hospital held these values on their computer for each item of food. We asked if we could visit them to obtain the information. We were able to get the details that we required but came across a pitfall that would sometimes plague businesses. A contractor had written the software for the hospital working alongside an NHS employee. Both had left and the staff remaining in the section had no idea how to operate the system effectively.

One area where the microcomputer proved an enormous asset to staff was when they had to write to schools. Most publications and letters were sent out in what became known as the school bag. Each school had a sack handled by 12 district administrative offices. These offices looked after local school matters such as admissions, exclusions and home to school transport. When a letter of a more urgent matter needed to be sent to schools, individual letters had to be put in the post to each. At that time there were about 640 primary, 120 secondary, 40 special and 40 nursery schools. If all schools were involved 840 or so names and addresses had to be entered onto envelopes. No sooner had they been put in the post something else would need to be sent and the procedure repeated rather like painting the Forth road bridge.

All the school names and addresses, reference numbers and other useful basic data were stored in a computer file. For the first time staff were able to print name and address labels for all schools or just those falling into particular categories such as being Church of England or those in the Lancaster area. Unlike the compact sheets of labels that you can easily buy at W.H. Smiths nowadays these labels were on continuous stationery. Occasionally a label would become detached and get itself stuck in the printer. It had to be scraped out with a knife or pair of scissors. Statistics could be readily obtained from the file such as the numbers and types of schools in each area or they could be printed to produce cross checking lists to tick when information had been returned.

People soon appreciated the benefits of these labels replacing what would have been the most tedious of jobs. Staff came up with their own ideas for setting up labels such as names and addresses of other local education authorities to which they had to write regularly. Another set comprised library, police and social services premises where the Playing Fields Service was responsible for maintaining flower beds or lawns.

Over the next few years a considerable list of tailor made applications were written for the DRS20 and an increasing number of machines linked to it. We regularly had to call out the engineers to replace boards in the computers or to remedy network problems, even with this limited set up. There were very little software packages around for these computers. One that was bought was called 'Demon Software' It was an early database but had the advantage that files could be easily created and information entered. At that time schools were beginning to buy their first photocopiers. A system to enable the section to easily record their details was produced in an hour or so using this software. Data could be exported and other specific programs written to provide analyses that were required.

One clever aspect of these machines was that filenames could have a privacy code at the end of the filename preceded by a single quotation mark. For instance the name may be DEMON'DCXX.

No one could see that part of the file name so that you could not just copy it from one machine to another. You could type simple commands to copy or delete files or show those in a directory. Files like the above would only appear as DEMON' so they could not be copied or removed without knowing the privacy code. To copy this software you had to run a program that requested a password. After you had entered it the file was copied but that password was no longer valid if you tried to run it again.

At this time each college of further education in Lancashire was obtaining minicomputers. These could manage larger networks than the micro computers and supported terminals that were used for both teaching purposes and administration. There were considerable debates about the merits of micros, minis and mainframes with each devotee favouring his or her preference that only a few years later would have the same relevance as thrashing out what model of black and white analogue television set you should buy for your home.

On one occasion an officer was delivering computers to Blackpool College. He parked his car as near to the entrance as possible in a reserved area, anticipating being there for only a few minutes whilst he unloaded the heavy equipment. Immediately someone came rushing up 'You can't park there, you can't park there. I'm on a course here, you can't park there!' Many people had become skilled at dealing with such outbursts and countered 'No doubt that will be a course on good manners and deportment!'

Blackpool College was an excellent place at which to attend meetings. It was noted for its first rate culinary facilities. After the gathering we would decamp to the principal's office where students on food preparation courses would provide a silver service including wine!

For the first time computers became available for home use. The Atari, Commodore PET and ZX Spectrums were early models. RAM consisted of maybe 32 kilobytes. The machines would read cassettes like those used by tape recorders at the time. Programs were loaded and data stored in this manner. Another popular machine was the Amstrad. There was a danger of a plethora of incompatible machines entering the market rather like railway companies building tracks with different gauges in the first half of the nineteenth century.

Many schools began to obtain a computer for teaching purposes. In order to create some consistency, to ensure that discounts were available for bulk orders and that staff were able to offer support and send machines for repair, RML models were adapted as the standard. Some schools had their own preferences and got into heated debates with specialist advisers. On one occasion after a discussion of some length the teacher attempted to end the argument with the words. 'Well you'll have to have you opinion and I'll have mine'. To which the adviser replied 'Madam, the County Treasurer pays me £16000 per year for my opinion, he pays you nothing. That represents the value of our respective opinions!'

Other types of machine started to appear in the office. One was known as a 'OnePer' short for One per desk. This was another ICL initiative. I felt that the company often had brilliant ideas but they were regularly overtaken by others and their products left floundering. The OnePers at Lancashire County Council were aimed at a handful of managers to evaluate. They enabled the users to store and send messages, had a diary and your own telephone directory and were linked to the telephone. One expert was asked to demonstrate the configuration to a 'volunteer user'. After showing what it could do to a somewhat cynical audience he pointed out that if you were not available to answer the telephone the machine could speak a message with vocabulary limited to words such as this, on, here and it for example. The manager created his own message so that the only output after a training session lasting 90 minutes or so was the following communication in the voice of a decrepit sounding dalek.

'I - have - gone - for - a - we - we!'

Some standardisation was to take place.

# 4

# THE ADVENT OF THE PC

During the mid nineteen eighties the department bought its first PC known as IBM Compatible. It was an ICL M30. This was a stand alone machine with its own hard disk drive with about 25 megabytes of space, on which to store files and software. Unlike the circular floppy disks on the DRS20 these machines had 3½ square diskettes that were to become the norm for many years.

The machines ran with the DOS operating system where you typed simple commands to perform everyday tasks such as to run programs, format diskettes or move files.

It was bought for a very specific purpose. This was to calculate the capacity of each school in line with a formula that the DES had devised. Spreadsheet software known as Supercalc-5 was bought. It was a new challenge to produce this system and quite different to set up formulae with built in functions and look up tables. A spreadsheet was created for each school giving details of the size and usage of every room and information about the roll. From this data and the formulae the capacity was calculated and in some cases would demonstrate that a school may be grossly under utilised.

A new printer was bought, with prices rapidly dropping. Cartridges had replaced the messy ribbons on previous models.

The machine could be located anywhere as it was not linked to anything. Other staff learnt how to set up spreadsheets of their own. For most this was the first occasion that they could use a computer to produce their own output and print-outs.

A handful of other simple spreadsheets were created for other sections such as dealing with pupils with special needs who went to schools outside the county or to the independent sector.

Several other offices bought a PC and developed their own applications. I was beginning to feel that I would be redundant but I was glad to say that they still came for assistance if required. Budget and Finance was a natural area where an allocation could be broken down into various areas and categories. The consequences of making changes or altering staffing numbers instantly showed the overall effect.

Two major changes happened to the department at this time. Most of the money allocated to the colleges of Further Education was withdrawn by the government. The colleges had to make a bid for the money by stating what courses they would run, the anticipated student numbers and reduction of duplication. A senior executive from one of the colleges was brought in to guide us through the period. I was asked to provide all sorts of statistics concerning course types and pupil numbers. It was literally cut and paste! Course details were cut out from one print-out and glued onto another sheet. The final outcome was a small group of staff running software on a mini computer, working on behalf of the colleges.

Even that set up only had a limited future. In the 1990s the colleges were funded directly from the Department for Education at Whitehall. The couple of programmers obtained employment writing software with private firms. The manager became a one-man business, working from his own premises to provide software and to put on training courses as required by the colleges.

The other change was the introduction of competitive tendering within the ancillary services of the education department. In particular these were in connection with school meals, cleaning and grounds maintenance. As is often the case consultants were brought in to investigate structures and make recommendations for the future.

Many of the senior staff in the services were very sceptical about consultants. They visited sites with the managers, had to ask them about every aspect and looked at our computer systems. They would be here for only a short time and did not have to carry the consequences of their proposals. They were also paid a lot more! It generated a new definition of the word Consultant.

'Someone who tells you what you already know and then charges for telling you!'

Of course there is also the joke about how many consultants it takes to change a light bulb – it depends how much money you've got in the budget! Alternatively none – they don't actually do anything they just tell you what you should be doing!

For the grounds maintenance in particular they requested that I wrote a substantial amount of software for them. Every location was identified. A drawing had to accompany each one. The number and size of every pitch to be prepared had to be provided, details of how they should be lined out and the number of times that they had to be mown each year. The area of flower beds to be hoed was included, hedges to be trimmed and even the compass markings that had to be drawn in the school yard.

The county was split into seven areas. Each had about 150 individual sites. A firm could bid for any or all of the seven areas. Potential contractors submitted their tender on a specific date.

For this first round of competitive tendering LCC won every contract for each business. However it was only going to be a matter of time before the private sector got its act together and started gaining them.

A consequence was that all the sections involved, along with certain others, where hived off to offices that had become available in Marsh Lane just down the road. Much of the programming work had been done on the DRS20 in County Hall and some on the new PCs. Although these former machines were obsolescent, the sections could not just drop the efforts that were held on them and bought a second hand DRS 20 from ICL. The data and programs were transferred.

The services themselves were each divided into the 'contractor', which did the work and formed the bulk of the staff and the 'client' who worked on behalf of the school or other service to ensure that the job was actually done. Theoretically an officer sitting at one desk could be haranguing another one at the next because the work had not been properly completed!

Over the following years external firms won most of these businesses and others from different departments such as vehicle maintenance. Under TUPE the staff all transferred to be employed by these new companies.

Later still all the contractor services were removed from their original departments within LCC and became DSOs (Direct Services Organisations). A few years down the line schools became free to choose whom they wanted to handle their businesses.

On the social side there was never a better time for those of us working for the council. The old staff canteens had closed during the 1970s to be replaced by two restaurants situated on the top floor of a new building. One was a sit down at a table with waitress service, the other a cheaper, self-service option. These were ideal for bringing guests who had travelled to come for a meeting or to take candidates who were being interviewed for vacancies. A bar and games room was situated behind the self-service refectory.

The whole area was known as the Staff Club. It was managed by a superb sports and entertainment committee. Football matches took place between departments – some able to field three teams – along with most other main sports. One large room had two table tennis tables. It could form an enjoyable evening's entertainment playing and then ending with a pint. You had to make sure that you avoided competition evenings when matches were played against other clubs. Snooker, pool and darts were similarly represented. A TV lounge was incorporated. I spent many a happy lunch time, taking my sandwiches to watch the test matches, in the days when there was full coverage of every ball on the BBC.

On Friday evenings in particular the bar area was packed out. Many retired members came back to the old haunt to meet up with old friends and acquaintances.

Lots of people booked the staff club to house special events such as birthdays of milestone ages. On many Saturday evenings there were live bands with dancing and hot pot suppers. Most departments arranged their own Christmas socials. One that I fondly remember was a games evening with more than a dozen teams of 4 competing against each other at table football, table tennis, darts, pool and dominoes.

Regular one-off events were arranged during the week. These might be a fashion show or a clairvoyant. One that was arranged to raise money for charity consisted of gaming tables, where you paid for chips to be used in the casino. We could pretend to be 007 on the blackjack, roulette or baccarat stands. On another occasion there was a murder mystery night. On that one I was asked to be one of the suspects. I didn't even know whether I had committed the crime or not! I just had to follow the script. On that instance there were some detectives taking part from Police HQ who did have an advantage.

Another popular evening was the quiz night. One consisting of teams of three was so well supported that twenty teams took part the first week, followed by a similar number the next. The leading ten teams from each heat met in a final later that month.

Quizzes had become fashionable in many pubs and clubs at that time. For a couple of years we put an LCC team into the local quiz league. The staff club tried to run a fun quiz once a fortnight but whilst initially well supported, numbers dwindled to a handful of teams.

Other groups met regularly. Once a week, at lunch time, a keep fit and aerobics class used the facilities. Every Wednesday night there was line dancing. One society that became well-established was a bridge club. Each Tuesday evening, excluding those few weeks such as Christmas when the building was closed, the group held a tournament. This carried on for years. I look back now with much sadness to these halcyon times when going to work wasn't merely a 20 mile rush setting out at an unearthly hour to get a parking space, a dash to avoid traffic jams on the return home with no further affinity with County Hall until the next day or ambitious people who were simply using Lancashire as a stepping stone towards their next promotion.

A very noticeable fact, whenever you attend a meeting of any club anywhere, is the age range of the participants. When the bridge club started out most members were in their forties and fifties. Twenty-odd years on the ages of those attending had risen similarly. New people had started coming but from the older end. Numbers began to decline as some had sadly passed away. This was the same with anything from travel societies to country dancing, concerts, choirs or slide shows on any topic. At a recent first-rate presentation at a college for adult education on the Yorkshire Dales including dinner, we looked round and only one couple looked younger than ourselves. Even they must have been 50! I often wonder what the future holds for groups like these. A local badminton club collapsed because of declining numbers – something that you would think was an attraction for younger participants. The staff club used to boast a very successful crown green bowling team. Whilst bowling was always regarded as an older person's pastime the squad ceased because of the lack of youth. At that time the captain of the side was in his early thirties but the average age was 72! What do young people actually do in their spare time?

One aspect of working that I had discovered was the enormous difference between a good manager and a poor one. This must be the most obvious of statements but when I started work I had the mistaken notion that all managers were in the positions that they were because they were able. Over the years I discovered that nothing could be farther from the truth. Whilst most were exceptionally capable and had progressed through the ranks because they had always done a good job and knew how to lead, others were there because they were determined to get to that spot. Often this meant flitting around the country, applying for posts at the next level as they became available. Manchester via the Midlands to London before returning to the North West might be an example of a route.

The weak managers were either sycophantic towards their superiors constantly stressing how great they were or alternatively were continually passing judgement on the way that things were run or wanted to change all that they had done with little regard for the consequences.

The good managers on the other hand respected their own bosses, stood up to them when needed and had meaningful meetings and discussions about how to tackle issues and make improvements. They were well-liked. Staff did their best for them so that there was seldom a need to upbraid anybody. If one of the team had made an error resulting in things going wrong their leader would go out of his/her way to help resolve it, give encouragement to the person who had made the mistake and find ways to best prevent a recurrence.

I found that the poor managers were only too eager to throw their weight around and undermine a decision made by their subordinates. When they had to confront an issue they often did not. One member of staff was considered to have taken excessive sick leave. The manager attempting to deal with the problem was informed 'You can't prove that I'm not sick!' And that was that.

There was a great difference in how they trusted their employees. The superior manager had faith that staff would get on with their job, asking them now and then how things were progressing. The staff happily consulted their manager if there was a difficulty or problem looming in the future, knowing that it would be dealt with.

Over the years there had been a great increase in the number of meetings held. As would be expected senior management teams held them at regular intervals but the rest of us only had them to discuss specific matters when required. Usually this was to determine and advise on what computer system a section required. In years gone by whenever an important issue had arisen an appropriate senior person would band us together and inform us.

When chairing a meeting good managers control it well. If people had drifted away from the topic under discussion, they would swiftly refocus. If they were not sure about a particular point they would say that and ensure that they found out the answer. They were more than happy to have attendees make wise cracks, tell anecdotes themselves and be the butt of jokes.

Weak managers were notoriously pompous. On the telephone they would always say this is Mr Dawson rather than Dawson or James Dawson for example. On one occasion a new chief officer had decided that we would become much more informal and everyone would be on first name terms. One reluctantly passed on this information but then added 'but I'm sure that you Sarah will want to continue to call me Mr Andrews!' They often blustered when they didn't know an answer rather than admit to it. A pet saying was 'I'll come back to that.'

Just in case you forgot they regularly had to remind everybody that they were the manager or 'that is a management issue.' One having such a feeling of superiority in himself asserted 'I have helicopter vision.' We couldn't resist asides – 'Whirl see about that', 'Blade into your hands', 'Uplifting experience.' They had a fondness for big words. 'Kudos' and 'Hubris' were frequent choices. Management-Speak phrases were common. Favourites were thinking outside the box, picking the low-hanging fruit, bringing it to the table, pushing the envelope and no-win situation. One member of the crew suggested that we make bingo cards with a selection of the most popular and mark them when they cropped up. If you completed a line you could shout 'Touch down!'

There was always the bad old joke 'What is the difference between a poor leader and a shopping trolley? The shopping trolley has a mind of its own!'

Delegated staff supplemented their pay with petrol money that they received when using their own car for official business. On one occasion a manager said that there was no mileage in going to a meeting in Leeds. That was merely setting himself up for the riposte 'Oh yes there's plenty of mileage in it, 140 miles at 39.6p a mile is 55 pounds 44 pence!' Whilst no-one should ever be out of pocket for using their vehicle it was regularly abused. One opportunist charged mileage for taking a parcel to the post office three hundred yards down the road for a pedestrian but over a mile there and back for a driver negotiating the one-way system.

Another officer commented that he was conscious of some matter or other. The chairman said 'Yes, yes I'm conscious of that too.' A wit piped up 'Well, just as long as we're all conscious!'

They had different ways of describing impending doom if things didn't go as planned or were delayed. One regularly would say 'when the balloon goes up.' Another had a much less eloquent choice of words 'when the shit hits the fan!'

At some meetings minutes were taken by an independent person who was not otherwise part of the discussions. One took place in September about financing school buildings. At the end of the meeting the chairman asked when she would be able to make the minutes available for circulation, expecting her to say tomorrow or the day after. 'November?' she suggested.

An anonymous individual had produced a poster. The gist of its message said 'Feeling Lonely in the Office?' 'Then arrange a meeting. Meet lots of people; write copious sheets of meaningless notes and above all – Feel Important.!'

Two further landmarks were taking place at this time. The first of these was the use of computers in school for administrative purposes. At this time there was an enormous gap in that area. We had written to each school to find out what software they were using. There was little common ground. Most were looking for some guidance and support. Noticing that there was a massive opening, a consortium comprising staff from schools, a local authority in the south of England and a private company provided a package from which any school could purchase a set of modules in the same way that you'd make a selection from an À la Carte menu. The central element was a record for each pupil but others that were available were for staff, examinations entry, timetables and finance. As there was an increasing need to have a word processing facility this was included in the bundle. The three standard ones at that time were Word Perfect, Word and Word Star. Word Star was chosen as the standard. Using this, schools discovered that they could easily create posters and notices for the corridor walls. All of this predated the introduction of Windows. In some schools two computers were linked together. One was to become known as the server and the other fed off that one. It could access files stored on either. The syndicate employed many more staff, moved to larger premises and were constantly developing the system in responses to user groups from schools around the country.

Another development was formula funding. In the past the Local Authority allocated a sum of money to each school to spend on books and materials. However all other funding and staffing levels were determined by the

Education Department based on pupil numbers, sometimes out of date, and perceived need. Schools in deprived areas would receive a higher amount for disadvantage. One suspected that in some areas (not Lancashire of course!) that senior education officials playing golf with some heads may have had a sympathetic ear to their requests for assistance.

From the early nineties almost all the potential schools budget would be devolved to the school. The Headteacher working with the School Governors would allocate the amount as they thought fit. In the ensuing years even more would be chipped away. The directive from the government was that the devolution should be formula based and transparent. We were assisted in this new role by a secondary and a primary headteacher. The formulae were straightforward, being based on the number of pupils in each year group, special needs factor calculated from the results of the screening test of 6 year old pupils for primary schools and those aged 11 at secondary and other factors such as if the school operated on more than one site. This generated everything from a basic allocation of the number of teachers and classroom support staff to the head teacher's salary.

As the great majority of the money in the authority was going to be devolved to the schools it was envisaged that there would be a need for considerably less staff. Consultants were called upon to make recommendations. Everyone completed job sheets of the work that they did over a fortnight. They then analysed these returns and made their proposals for the department. As I recall these were to lose 60 posts in the first year followed by 100 in the second. The 12 district offices would be disbanded but would be replaced by a larger number of 'Information Offices.' These resource centres would be scattered throughout the county. They could be housed anywhere such as in libraries or citizens advice offices. Any member of the public would be able to go to one of these locations to find out about local schools, see if they were eligible for a clothing allowance or how to appeal against a decision about which school their child was to be admitted.

In fact none of their recommendations actually happened. The twelve district offices were reduced to six. Instead of cutting staff numbers their functions were made available to schools to purchase if they wished. For example as part of the formula, money was devolved to each school for the governing body, including training and the clerking of meetings. Schools could organise their own if they desired. Alternatively they could buy them back from the area office. Another scheme enabled them to buy the services of an IT Support Centre that would look after the schools system and provide sessions with a tutor. If schools did not wish to procure services such as these, staff numbers would be reduced. In fact most schools have taken them up and have been very happy with them. Staff numbers have been maintained or actually increased.

With prices dropping, computers were turning up throughout the department. The decision was taken to cable every section so that each PC would be linked to a server located in the IT Division in Treasurers Dept and maintained by them. They would ensure that back-ups of all the data were performed every evening. The server would have about a gigabyte of storage, 1000 million characters and could support 100 PCs logged on to it. No-one could envisage filling all the available space.

The IT Division itself had undergone a major reorganisation. Long gone were the days of rigid compartments of systems analysts, programmers or punch room staff. The thrust had changed to development teams and support staff.

This was the start of a period of phenomenal growth in the size and speed of computers and the reductions in price that nobody could have foreseen. Not long before, the Police had bought a huge server with 3000 megabytes of storage to hold details of every incident. This was regarded as colossal at the time. Now PCs, printer and photocopiers were being obtained by the lorry load. Offices could purchase their own without having to first set aside funds to pay for them. A machine would be bought one month that had say 80 megabytes of storage. The next month 150 was standard. Soon it was 450. A few years later there was more disk space on the local machine than on the entire network! There was a similar exponential growth in the memory available whenever new machines were acquired. There was little leadership or control in the purchases. They were springing up like weeds. The time was rapidly approaching when there was a computer on every desk.

A system would be written. It was then discovered that it would not work on a customer's PC because it was over a year old and did not have sufficient memory. Money would regularly have to be found for an upgrade. A spreadsheet could operate on one machine in an office but not another. Others would not work because the various PCs were set up with different settings. Even worse was that the limit of 100 PCs linked to the server was frequently being breached. As staff increasingly had most of their files stored on the server, this preventing them from getting on with their work.

It was so frustrating that one colleague remarked whilst standing in the gents 'You know Peter, this is the one room in the building where everybody knows what they're doing!' Another produced a comic strip that compared the crews in the varsity boat race working in unison with the cox shouting through a load speaker to that at Lancashire where there was one rower and eight people bawling different instructions!

This was summed up when I received a memo asking for advice. As it was a matter that required input from a higher level I passed it on to a person of more seniority. A week later, the memo having passed right round the circuit with half a dozen names on it came back to me asking for guidance!

A notice read 'The light at the end of the tunnel has just gone out!'

Since the earliest days of computing there had only been a handful of standard programming languages and operating systems. When PCs hit the market DOS was the norm. None of this was to last. Any software that was bought had its own built-in language. To know all the ins and outs of Supercalc including automating tasks via macros was a quest in itself. Databases became a fashionable word with Dbase software being used. In no time there was Foxpro, Ingres, Pascal, Oracle and Clipper. When COBOL was the mainstay, newcomers making amendments to existing programs and writing their own, used to be employed for two years before you could say that they were competent. Now new products were being thrown at people who were expected to get to grips with them instantly.

Another product had been introduced by ICL. This was known as Office Power. This was an early form of electronic communication that had it own word processing facility. Unfortunately this was a product that arrived before Microsoft Office had begun to really hit the market. The screen did not show what the message or documents would actually look like when they were printed. Some staff were quite keen to use it and arranged a meeting and sent out details by this method. However there was no guarantee that the people to whom it was sent were actually using it and they didn't turn up. On another occasion after information had been sent in this way a clerk had to telephone all the intended recipients to determine if they had opened the correspondence! This was a classic case of using technology for technology's sake. Instead of a tool to save time and money it did exactly the opposite.

One department went in for it in a big way decreeing that all staff would use it. The problem was that things were changing so rapidly that they would soon be left with it as a millstone whilst others were replacing their limited use with more state of the art commodities.

One of the government's flagships had been to reorganize local government so that there would only be 'Unitary Authorities.' These would replace the system whereby local government functions were divided between county councils and district councils. This would have made things easier for the public. For example we once reported a footbridge in need of repair but it was never clear who was responsible for it.

A county that was looked at in the early days was Derbyshire. The recommendation was that there would be only two councils Derby City Council and Derbyshire County Council taking care of the rest and thus removing all the other districts. There was much outcry. Proposals for Lancashire included a break up into six or seven councils covering the main conurbations such as merging Preston and South Ribble and the councils of East Lancashire. It was opposed by Lancashire and those councils that would lose out but supported by those that would gain. Local opinion was also sought. This episode resulted in maintaining the status quo for Lancashire as it did for many other regions. A few were changed. For instance Berkshire was abolished, its functions being taken over by larger borough councils. For the time being Lancashire carried on as before.

## 5

## THE NINETEEN NINETIES

Even more far reaching events were taking place. Computers were still largely driven by typing in commands or making selections from a menu by using the arrow keys. The latest purchases came with 'Windows' built in. In future all programs would be windows based where you were prompted for what you wanted to do with a list or selection of icons and you merely clicked the required choice with a mouse.

Alongside this came Microsoft Office. A number of utilities came with it but the main ones were Word, Excel and Access. Vast numbers of people were buying PCs with Windows for their home use. For under £1000 their machines at home were more powerful than those that they used every day in the office, had more storage and were easier to use. Suddenly systems at work seemed archaic.

'Word' became the standard for the production of reports. The fact that it was simple to use, you could see on the screen what the final presentation would look like and could change the size and format of letters, words or whole blocks made it a world beater. As you used it more you discovered that you could set up tables and formulae, import pictures, graphs or blocks from other programs. What a godsend that would have been more than 20 years earlier at university when post graduates had to pay scribes who would type up their theses. When you compared this to the limitations of other software everyone wanted to change. This had an effect on the tying pool. Many senior officers discovered that rather that write out a report for a secretary or typist to enter they could save time by doing it themselves. They could review it as they typed and make fine alterations that wouldn't have been practicable if someone else was doing it on their behalf. Many had bought a laptop so they could work at home or any other location.

'Access' turned into the database program. Again as you became familiar with it you discovered that it could do anything that you wanted including linking to files belonging to other software. 'Excel' was the replacement for 'Supercalc.' Microsoft Outlook (formerly Express) took over as the universal method of electronic communication or email sweeping its predecessors under the carpet.

All sorts of people that had never previously had any involvement with computers regarded themselves as experts and wanted a database for their own particular aspect of work. Noting this, I'm sure a computer magazine won't mind me quoting a cartoon that had a so called expert going to the head of development. 'I want a database.' 'Oh no, not another one' he thought. Then with a wry smile he asked 'What colour would you want for you database?' After some thought the customer suggested 'I believe that mauve has the most RAM!'

Although there had been no change to the boroughs and county of Lancashire, investigators had discovered that the voting in Blackpool and Blackburn had been less extreme than other areas in its opposition to change. The whole proposals were revisited. Those two councils did wish to 'go it alone' feeling that they could work better for their towns and communities on their own, obtain external income to regenerate blighted areas and campaigned for their independence. This was approved. These new councils would look after services such as education locally. They would be taken away from Lancashire for their areas. The effect was to take out about one sixth of Lancashire and the need to remove at least one post in six.

In some respects this was the worst scenario. Lancashire still existed albeit reduced, twelve district councils carried on as before and these two boroughs expanded requiring chief officers to take charge of the new services. Many of us have pondered what the situation would have been like if Lancashire had been disbanded and there had been authorities consisting of Fylde, Blackpool and Wyre, Central Lancashire (Preston, South Ribble and Chorley) and East Lancs. West Lancashire might have amalgamated with Southport and Lancaster with the southern Lake District.

One of the most straightforward methods of reducing staff was to determine those who wished to take redundancy. On this unusual occasion generous terms were offered. Some people who were totally dissatisfied with their current jobs took the opportunity of the severance pay. If their position could be deleted from the establishment those people who were over 50 years were allowed to retire and would receive their pension early. A letter was sent to people in that age group asking if they were interested in departing under these terms and if so how many months notice would they require before they would be prepared to leave.

Some could not wait to finish. In response to the correspondence one colleague replied 'Would this afternoon be soon enough?' At the other extreme some staff approaching sixty did not wish to go. However one was issued with the threat 'Well, shall I make someone of 40 redundant?'

Because sections had to be created in the new councils for such matters as admitting pupils to schools and special educational needs they were very willing to take staff with this expertise from Lancashire. This was especially useful to those who lived in East Lancashire or on the Fylde coast.

As section heads and chief officers could not be split into sixths, departments were merged and the six former Area Offices were now reduced to three. The Planning and Surveyors Departments merged to become the Environment Directorate. Education and Libraries combined to form Education and Cultural Services. This also incorporated the Records Office and Museums Service.

Computer systems were also changing rapidly. Big corporate systems written by software companies that ran on large servers and accessible from any location were replacing those systems operating in the department. Because they were written for use by many companies across Britain everyone had to fit in with them. Every educational establishment was expected to have a DFE number even if it did not have one. It would have to be invented before it would be accepted. That was all very well until a real one cropped up with that number. Other systems commissioned from the IT Department had now to be properly priced and went ahead only if there was a business case and money in an appropriate budget.

It is hard to credit nowadays that mobile phones were only just hitting the market. Initially they were quite cumbersome objects being first obtained by the elite. Land line telephones had barely improved for decades. The only real change had been the conversion of the rotary dial where you put your fingers in the holes to today's key pad. The ring tone was much the same as it was years before. Enhancements were few and far between such as 1471 and 1571 to see who last called you and to allow a message to be left if you were not there to answer it.

The vast explosion, especially with 'Pay as you go' happened in only a couple of years. I often wonder why things that were automatically included such as showing missed calls, sending and receiving text messages and the ability to hold all the numbers that you regularly rang with their names could not have been made available on conventional phones fitted with a little screen.

Mobiles became a blessing when you think of occasions such as the car breaking down and the struggle to find a phone booth to contact the motoring organizations or to be stuck in a delayed train being unable to contact your family but became a headache to teachers when pupils sent text messages in lessons and later used their phones to take photos that they sent to their friends.

Computer networks were upgraded. Disk capacity increased and the restrictions in the number of users that could be logged on to the network at any time were removed. Printers had changed out of all recognition.

Instead of merely printing lines of figures or documents all of a sudden first class booklets with diagrams and quality colour photographs could be produced. The combination of corporate systems being obtained for financial and personnel services, packages being bought in to replace many that I had previously provided and the ease by which staff could produce their own work with Office products meant that the job that I had done for years was no longer the same. I contemplated taking redundancy myself and looking for alternative employment. Instead I took the opportunity of making a move to a part that was to become known as the 'Advisory Division' of the Education Department.

This was an area where most staff worked directly with schools. This included areas such as inspections, collection of test results and going into schools that were having problems.

Many stories came from people visiting the schools. So many books of delightful tales have been produced that I've only included a few.

One youngster was asked how he liked his school. 'Closed!' he replied - a punch line worthy of many a stand-up comedian. Another had just completed his first day in the reception class. His father asked how he had enjoyed the occasion. 'It was all right, but I don't think I'll join' he replied in all seriousness!

In the 1950s our first reading books introduced us to Dick and Dora, Nip the dog and Fluff the cat. These are still in use today. During assembly a hymn was being sung with a line 'God whose name is love'. One little girl who hadn't heard it properly was singing in a loud voice 'Dog whose name is Fluff.' The teacher pointed this out. 'Those aren't the right words Jenny.' She answered 'Yes, I didn't think they were – the cat is Fluff!'

On a different occasion the numbers of the hymns to be sung that day were shown on a board. The teacher asked if anybody knew what the numbers meant. One boy confidently put his hand up and asserted 'It's Jesus' mobile number!'

In the classroom the teacher and all the pupils were stood in a big ring holding hands ready to play a game. One lad asked if he could go to the toilet. On his return he took up his position next to the teacher and held her hand. Noticing that it was still wet the teacher pointed out 'Make sure that you dry your hands after you've been to the toilet Steven.' 'I didn't wash my hands miss!'

During a numeracy lesson the class had been learning about more than and less than. 'Can anybody give me an example about how we would use more than?' 'My uncle lives in more than Ireland!'

A photograph was being taken of the whole class. One pupil could not see why anyone should want the picture.

The teacher explained that in many years time you'll be able to say that they were my friends and she's a doctor now and he's an architect. Yes and I'll be able to say that's the teacher – she's dead!

One child was very upset because a boy in the class had said that her mother was a prostitute. She went to the teacher to complain about his remarks. 'But she isn't sir, she's a catholic!'

An example of word confusion happened just outside the building. A motorcyclist skidded and came off his bike. A bystander looked horrified when his helmet rolled into the road until he got up none the worse for his ordeal and commented 'For a minute I thought that he'd been decaffeinated!'

A growing area at this time was the need to be able to provide information from data that was held on computer files. Instead of having a series of reports as was the case in the past, it was necessary to be able to interrogate sets of data and link them together in response to requests from councilors, chief officers and advisers. One brief was to have figures at our fingertips so that advisers would be aware if a school was in difficulties, well before it was inspected and put into a 'Special Measures' or 'Serious Weaknesses' category. Schools that were would be given a length of time to improve. They would be given additional resources to assist with this but after a period if they had not improved could even be closed.

During the nineties schools had been split into a foundation stage for the reception class and key stages 1 – 4. Literacy and numeracy hours had been introduced along with assessments or test at then end of each key stage. Whilst those for 11, 14 and 16 year old pupils were externally marked those for 7 year old pupils were dealt with in the school. A recent development had been the need to collect and analyze all these results that were received from different locations.

The Key Stage 1 results at the end of year 2 had to be collected from each school that had any children of this age group. Initially forms from schools were entered into a machine that could optically read lines on special stationery. This was a laborious and error prone method of obtaining the figures. It was a useful and easy to operate method if you only required a sample of answers – such as what attendees felt about the facilities at a venue for a conference – but not when you had to have the exact values for every child. Instead we worked with a headteacher to provide a program that could be loaded onto a computer in every school and the results entered in a simple manner. After rigorous testing, several hundred floppy disks were shipped out to schools along with guidance notes and each returned the results that were then loaded into our systems.

Many schools were not very familiar with computers at this time and did not know how to load a floppy disk. At a later stage we had to send upgrades to certain schools that did not have particular software available, to enable them to print out the results. These were distributed on CDs. One school secretary informed us that their machine did not have a facility to read a CD. When we pointed out that there was a little button that they could press and a mechanism in which to place the compact disc would shoot out, she told us that she thought that the device was a coffee cup holder!

Over the years the methods were developed further. The original system was improved to become windows based. Schools were able to produce the data from their own 'school information systems' thus removing the need to send them programs. A further improvement was to be able to send the results automatically by the click of a button rater than writing them to a floppy disk that was put in the post or delivered to the building.

The Key Stage 2 and 3 results were sent to us from the Qualifications and Curriculum authority on a CD.

One area of which we were completely unaccustomed was the setting of targets. These were very popular with the new government in all aspects of life. The first targets were the percentage of pupils achieving level 4 or better in English, mathematics and science at Key Stage 2 and attaining 5 or more grades A* - C at GCSE. The authority had to set targets for the whole of its area. Each school had to set its own targets. Each school had these aggregated, weighted by the number of pupils to determine if it met those that the LA had set. The purpose of the targets was to help improve schools. Whilst targets on their own would not do this it ensured that teachers would look at every individual pupil to ascertain what could be achieved.

The Authority had to help schools set targets and advisers had to challenge those schools where they were not sufficiently 'aspirational.' Those schools that had not set them by a specific date each year had to be contacted. Some became quite shirty. One adviser asked to speak to the head. 'This is Geoff Dutton speaking - could I speak with Mr. Ambrose please?' 'We don't have a Mr. Ambrose.' 'Oh, I could have sworn that I received a letter from Mr. Ambrose.' 'We do have a Dr Ambrose.' 'Then could you kindly tell Dr Ambrose that Dr Dutton wishes to speak with him!'

There was ridiculous talk once that a school could be closed for not reaching its targets. As these were set by a voluntary governing body and pupils could be sick or on holiday in Florida at the time of the tests it was soon dismissed. In recent years schools have to have a SIP (School Improvement Partner) to help them set targets.

Once all the targets had been collected they were sent to the Department for Education where they would be compared at the appropriate time with the actual results. That department had frequently altered its name over the last decade. For many years it was known as the DES

(Department for Education and Science). That became the DfEE (Department for Education and Employment). Next was DfES (Department for Education and Skills). More recently this has changed again to DCSF (Department for Children, Schools and Families). This acronym was quite difficult to remember until somebody thought of the mnemonic 'Department for Carpets and Soft Furnishings!'

The department had its own share of pomposity. They were once speaking to a head of service, querying some results. Their employee wanted him to put him in touch with a statistician – stating after all, what would you know about figures? 'Would a PhD in statistics be sufficient?' he answered.

Over the years additional targets had to be gathered for key stage 3 results and absence. Very recently the thrust has changed from pupils achieving the expected level for their age group to attaining that in both English and mathematics. The other development has been to set them for pupils moving up two levels. This would apply to children of all abilities to ensure that they all continued to progress throughout their schooling.

At this time many firms chose to have a mission statement to sum up the purpose and values of their business. It was a brief proclamation regarding what they were about. For example that of Microsoft was 'To enable people and businesses throughout the world to realize their full potential.' EasyJet - To provide our customers with safe, good value, point-to-point air services.

Parts of the council developed their own. That of our section became 'Leading in the provision of accurate educational data.' We were so often bombarded with requests for what was sometimes unnecessary information that we devised our own 'Alternative Statements.' In fact the greatest aspects of going to the office or factory to relieve the grind were your companions in the work place, the excellent humour and general banter.

We felt that the desire for excellence was over ambitious so instead we had 'We strive for adequacy!' From this there soon became a list of mottos.

Sometimes information might be different depending upon how you interpreted certain areas. A customer believed that the figures provided were less than exact so we listed 'We are not as wrong as we could be!'

Written on the board was 1 4 0 and 0 4 1. This was merely so that visitors would ask what it meant 'One for all and all for one!' We didn't like to be too serious.

Some customers even came to the office with their own suggestions. One who had been told at a meeting that she must not pass on anything from the discussion added 'I've been told not to repeat this so I'm only going to say it once!' Some senior officers could not resist disclosing things that they shouldn't and warned us to keep it between these four walls. We could not resist the following 'You must treat this as very confidential – as I was saying to the cleaner!'

Regularly schools complained that the information that we had provided for them was incorrect. We checked the data and more often than not found that we were right and that the school had overlooked something. This created another adage 'The customer is always wrong!'

To avoid being found out two more became 'When in doubt – throw it out!' and 'Destroy the evidence.'

If you made the mistake of arriving early you could almost guarantee that a head of service would be hovering having found a mistake or wanting yet more figures. More aphorisms were consequently added to the board. 'He who makes no mistakes isn't working hard enough!' 'The early bird catches the blame!' For those people who didn't gripe about receiving additional jobs 'Blessed are the meek – for they shall inherit the work!' As an antithesis to Harry S Truman – 'The buck doesn't stop here!'

To ensure that you were not over stretched 'We set our targets low – so we are seldom disappointed!' We received a succession of visitors to the office. 'Everyone brings joy to the office when they arrive – or as they leave!' To provide a pretext to enable us to chat we borrowed an advertisement from BT – 'It's good to talk!'

A final message had more than an element of truth in it. Schools that were achieving less well than others regularly received pots of money from various sources to help bring them up to scratch that the more successful ones did not. 'We penalise success!'

School inspections themselves have undergone major overhaul over the past ten years. Originally schools were told a couple of months in advance that they were to be inspected. This would enable some to disguise those areas where they felt vulnerable. In 2005 this would change to a couple of days notice. Each aspect that was inspected was originally graded 1 to 7 (Excellent to completely inadequate) to just four grades nowadays - 1 Excellent, 2 Good, 3 Adequate and 4 Inadequate. Items inspected all fitted into the Every Child Matters agenda. Amongst the features investigated were the achievements of each key stage, leadership, using assessment data, attendance, the quality of the teaching and to ensure that the school had improved since its previous inspection. Schools had to show that they had consulted with their stake-holders – pupils and their parents and guardians.

Over the previous ten years schools had been able to choose who provided those functions to assist with its day to day running. A recent initiative had been the creation of services that schools were free to decide whether or not to partake. They had to be self-financing. One that had been available for some time had been the option to buy into in-service training courses.

'Value-added' was something that we had developed that schools were happy to pay for. This basically compared their previous results to those of the most recent examinations. It measured pupils' progress to those of Lancashire schools as a whole and made an attempt to predict the most likely grade that each pupil would attain at GCSE in the various subjects.

Other enterprises were pupil questionnaires that explored their attitudes in a number of areas and compared opinions split by gender and year group with the averages for the project. Many schools took steps to make improvements in those areas where they fared less well than they might have hoped. A parent questionnaire also operated where schools could select questions that were pertinent to them. A bonus was the fact that some schools outside the authority bought into these ventures. Schools used the results from these analyses to demonstrate that they had consulted with customers as required when inspected and had acted upon the findings.

Much emphasis was placed on teaching children with special educational needs. There was a whole spectrum of SEN varying from visual or hearing impairment, learning difficulties ranging from moderate to severe and profound to complex areas such as those with autism. We had training from experts in the field where we wore specially made spectacles that showed us exactly what it was like to have partial or defective sight. A group of people developed a system, known as PIVATS, to recognize small scale measurable improvements in each field that these pupils could be compared against. These folders became so popular that they were sold in hundreds not only to schools across the British Isles but also world wide to establishments in Singapore, Australia and the Falkland Islands.

Pupils with learning difficulties had individual development plans with stepping stones of anticipated improvements. They received intense help to try to attain these small steps. Some made such excellent progress with this individual help that their original statement of special need could be removed.

The handling of this area had made giant leaps. Even in the sixties children were put into groups for 'retards.' Words such as idiot that are regularly used for anybody behaving in a stupid manner had very specific medical definitions a hundred years ago. People were grouped into horrible sounding categories like cretin or imbecile. A speaker joked that if in use today the pupil's statement of possible progress might read 'If he continues to make this excellent progress he'll no longer be an idiot, he'll be a moron!'

Great strides were also made across the buildings to assist staff with disabilities. These could be anything from small scale stair lifts to carry a wheel chair to magnified screens to help employees with poor vision. Things had progressed substantially in only a short time.

# 6

# THE TWENTY FIRST CENTURY

A very popular occasion was the leaving do. Over the years I must have been to dozens if not hundreds of these. Most of these were people who had been with the county council for a few years and were moving on for a promotion, a change in direction or in recent years to go travelling. This year away roving the world is so fashionable amongst youngsters these days, who often worked for two or three years after finishing at university to earn enough money for the trip, as to have become the norm. This was not an option in our day. Even the 'European Rail Card', for the under 25s only became available in the late nineteen seventies. The World Travel, often starting in America and always including a long stay in Australia and New Zealand before finishing in eastern Asia is the usual schedule with details sorted out by travel agents. Although dominated by young people in their twenties, my daughters whilst away backpacking assured us that there were many people in their sixties travelling. The difference was that they tend not to 'rough it' preferring to stay in hotels, having a desire for comfort rather than cheapness. There is hope for us yet!

At some periods in the eighties salaries for computer staff were comparatively low when compared with private industry and there were often two or three leaving sessions in a month. For some people going to a leaving do was an opportunity to have some free booze, a snack and a chat. It was almost like finding out about a party and gate crashing! Sometimes you tagged along because a friend was going. I remember attending one – somebody that I had never met and shook hands saying 'It's been very nice knowing you Derek.' 'No - Donald.' 'Sorry it's been very nice knowing you Donald!'

At another there was a queue of about twenty people waiting for a glass of wine. I was at the back and reached over and was passed one. A colleague near the front who had been waiting for ten minutes commented 'What's he got that I haven't?' I couldn't resist the reply 'A glass of wine!'

By far the best leaving does where the ones were staff retiring aged 60 or over who had been here since leaving school at 16. They had remarkable stories. One that I recall from some years ago was from a man that had started at the county council in 1949. He spoke about his duties in those early days. Three main tasks were

Making the fires in the morning! That was hard enough at home if the wood on top of the paper didn't take hold sufficiently to light the coal. Once the fires were roaring toast could be made by holding slices of bread on long forks over the flames.

Going the rounds filling inkwells. This was long before mod cons such as the fountain or cartridge pen. Blotches of ink regularly used to be found on people's work. Not many employees would even know what blotting paper was that was used to soak up the stains!

Putting oil into officers' cigarette lighters! Many junior staff had to go out to the shop across the road to buy cigarettes for their seniors. Now that smoking is banned from all public places this is the most incredible of all.

We tend to think that topics such as recycling and conservation are modern initiatives. However in the 1960s obtaining stationery was extraordinarily difficult. You were issued with a pen and pencil from an appropriate person (like the chalk monitor at school) and would only be replaced when the pen had run out or the pencil consisted of a stub. That was not even the end of it. A nib was issued, resembling a cigarette holder from a Noel Coward play, in which to insert the pencil stub thus extending its life! Rubbers were cut into a minimum of two pieces.

The office hierarchy was taken to extremes. A junior auditor had a stamp with his number that he used when figures had been checked. More senior officers had stamps with their initials. When a new officer started with initials PW rather than spend anything on a new stamp a bit was broken off from the RW design to instantly provide a PW. What value for money!

People starting at 16 had no thought whatsoever about leaving or applying for other jobs. Most started work on a Scale 1 in the General Office. They would perform wonderfully fulfilling tasks such as assembling documents for meetings and placing them in envelopes. After a couple of years there might be a vacancy for a Scale 1/2 in another section and so on. There were no job applications. Somehow people knew when it was their turn. If you'd be there the longest on a particular grade, unless you'd made a great hash of things, it was your turn next. You'd make a very gradual but steady climb to a more senior post.

At a recent retirement do an officer left aged 60 having started in 1965. He gave us details of office outings at the time. A coach trip would be organized for men only! This would be an afternoon visit to a pub with a bowling green. He told us that female staff had their office trip – to a slipper factory in Rossendale. The nineteen-sixties was a time of sexual liberation and one lady did not see why only the men could go drinking and bowling and decided that in future, an excursion would be open to men and women. It was. The following year men and women went on the same trip - to the slipper factory!

One of the nicest aspects of the leaving do was that staff who had worked with the person retiring were invited back. We could mingle with people that we had not seen for a number of years. Most looked as fit as a fiddle and sported a Mediterranean like suntan. On this occasion a man returned, aged 88, who had been retired 28 years – before some of the younger colleagues were born. One recurrent theme that each had was that they don't know had they could possibly have had time to come to work!

One of the saddest losses in the 21st century was the final decline of the staff club amenities. This had begun in the nineties with the closure of the 'Waitress Service' refectory and the original television room. The TV moved to an area next to the bar. Next to go was the former table tennis room, recently used for general meetings. The main self-service restaurant closed. There had been a steady decline in its use over the last 20 years. Most people had changed to having a snack or sandwich for lunch but it was still a disappointment to the staff who did use it regularly. An open plan office replaced the restaurant and a small-scale Internet cafe selling snacks along with a drinks and newspaper shop opened in the old building. After much deliberation it was decided to retain the bar and games area, provide a new dance floor and to refurbish the seating. In all fairness an effort was made to try to promote the bar and facilities.

We knew that the inevitable would happen at some time. The two snooker tables were used only by a few aficionados. Ten years before there was a waiting list every lunchtime. Now there were single figure entries in the pool competitions. On some Tuesday evenings when I had returned to watch a sky television football match only a handful of us had replaced the two dozen or more that would have been there in earlier years. Just one person had been kept on to run the bar. Even on the last day before the Christmas break the room was empty, staff preferring to drink at hostelries in the city centre rather than support the traditional spot. The photographs below show the staff club in its death throes.

A forlorn barman in the last few weeks before the staff club closed.

Not as busy as in its hey day, but the snooker and pool tables were always well-used.

Following its closure everything was auctioned. This included items ranging from snooker chalk, darts and cutlery to Xmas decorations, bar stools and the snooker tables themselves. This area is now also office accommodation. R.I.P.

Over the past few years the number of meetings had seemed to grow inexorably. Unlike in previous years they were held at monthly intervals for 'awareness' or 'keeping in touch' purposes. Officers were drawn from different parts of the county for a meeting that might last only an hour but would disrupt at least half a day. Information packs were given to each attendee that at best would find their way to the recycling box. They had the effect of taking staff away from the job that they should have been doing. There was plenty of truth in the sketch where the manager is addressing his senior staff with the words 'There is not enough work being done and we're going to meet every morning until we find out why!'

'Away Days' and 'Service Days' had become popular. A short time prior to their taking place people were regularly asked for ideas for the agenda. There was a dichotomy of opinion between the employees that embraced outings like these and those who would run a mile to avoid them.

Groups were constantly undergoing reorganization or realignment. The former Social Services Department had been split. Provision for adult care was separated from services for children which combined with the Education and Cultural Service to form a new directorate that became known as Children and Young People along the lines of the DCSF.

Many firms could see that there was a market in the use of assessment data, analysis of examination results and methods of setting targets. Web sites were springing up that enabled schools to scrutinise their results to determine if pupils had made the progress that might be expected of them.

This was the start of an era of great frustration for schools and everyone else involved with 'login and password meltdown.' We had all become used to digital locks where you press four numbers to open a door or enter your pin code to get money from automated teller machines at various outlets. When you logged onto your computer you would enter a simple password – usually the name of your cat or football team.

A system called Raise on-line that became known as 'Rage On-line' as headteachers pulled out their hair in anguish! Quite apart from the system regularly breaking down you were given a log-in consisting of 8 characters – a mixture of digits, upper and lower case letters. An example might be rJj3uR7v. The correct case had to be entered. You were also presented with an equally meaningless password that you were invited to change (but it had to be 8 characters long with at least one numeral, capital and small letter).

Another web site that schools had to use to request additional time fo help certain pupils complete their SATs papers had similar but different codes. Many heads could not log in to the systems and became exasperated at having to ring the LA to request a new password. This was barely confidential data to help a pupil who might have impaired hand movement do well in a test. There seemed to be an obsession with secrecy whilst something as simple as a four digit number would enable you buy goods costing £1000.

Major developments were taking place that involved the combining of sections into 'Corporate Images.' Until then there had been separate offices in the different departments dealing with such matters as finance. The policy now was to combine these into one service, with one overall manager.

Change was never favoured at the best of times. In fact a poster on an office wall read 'The only person that likes change is a wet baby!'

Until then each department had its personnel sections. In recent years this was known as HR or Human Resources. This was popularly branded 'Human Remains.' All these sections from around the county were combined along with payroll, pensions, training and Health & Safety functions to become Lancashire Pay Services. The intention was to centralise these services, remove duplication and cut down on staff numbers.

Vacancies were not filled. Many members of staff were unwilling to move and resigned or sought employment elsewhere. Some others who accepted the move did not like the new conditions and subsequently handed in their notice. Certain posts could not be filled at all. In common with most companies the solution was to have yet another reorganisation. As one colleague quipped 'It's like reshuffling the deck chairs on the Titanic!' This resulted in some staff being pensioned off at a couple of weeks notice.

A further development was the intention to perform all communications electronically to what would become known as 'The Paperless Society.' Within the county information was provided by way of the Intranet. There were some excellent aspects such as the On-line Telephone Directory that enabled you to contact any employee with up-to-date details – something that would not have been possible with conventional directories and address books. All vacancies were listed along with the location of all establishments in Lancashire.

The portal was a method devised to allow communication to and from schools. Instead of the surfeit of letters, booklets and information packs with which schools were constantly bombarded these were to be all placed onto this new website resembling an email. Some of these could be simply read and dismissed or deleted. Others allowed the school to place a tick or cross to show whether or not they were willing to partake in a scheme for example. As with many things in the early days this had not been particularly successful.

A very recent development enables the school to select an electronic form for certain statutory duties on which they provide figures or details. They could also choose to buy into projects and select various options by this method. This replaced the need to complete a manual form to be posted or faxed later. Previously details would have then been entered by clerical staff into a computer system with the inherent errors that could be expected. Now methods could be found that would upload this information from the schools without the need for manual intervention. These solutions represented real savings and improvements in efficiency.

# 7

# RECENT EVENTS

One problem that has sometimes occurred in recent years has been the filling of posts. This has often resulted from the method that jobs have to be advertised. In the 1990s much work was done to comply with equal opportunities legislation. These were obviously good laws to ensure that there was no discrimination in employment because of such things as gender, ethnicity or disability. However in the past, under normal circumstances vacancies were first advertised internally. If there were no suitable applicants they were then put into the newspapers and local government press. This was changed to comply with Equal Ops. Recently posts have been advertised nationally from the outset. Naturally, internal aspirants could also apply. A temporary appointment for a data analyst was advertised in this manner. Candidates were sieved and a short list set up. Some did not turn up for the interview at all. The position was offered to the most suitable. The person said that he would accept. When formal notification was sent to him there was no reply. It seemed that he was holding out, awaiting a result of an application to a different firm.

Weeks later the whole process was repeated. This time it was apparent that the successful contender was merely using this as a lever to persuade her existing employer to give her a pay rise. It worked, she did get an increase.

Adverts nowadays stipulate essential and desirable criteria. Applicants are scored not only on their answers to these points but also on the evidence that they specify. The result has regularly been that some people are 'good at playing the game.' They attend the right courses, know what to enter onto the form to put themselves forward often at the expense of others who do not sell themselves as effectively, don't score so highly and consequently do not get an interview even though they may be much more suited to the vacancy.

These candidates are short listed and interviewed. Sometimes they have had to be offered the post because they fared better than the others even though the persons conducting the interview had a sense that he or she would not fit well with the rest of the section. That gut-feeling often proved to be correct. In days gone by they would not have been taken on. Those not appointed or even interviewed have the right to request feedback about their lack of success. It was often a long conversation where the applicant grilled the person conducting the interview about every topic on the form causing stress all round. Some have complained to a higher level. Things have moved some distance since the early seventies when part of one discussion at an interview compared the qualities of Preston North End to those of Sheffield Wednesday or when a boss passed a member of his team on the corridor and said 'You're starting in Section 9 on Monday!'

On many occasions when staff resigned from their post someone from another section filled the job temporarily whilst its duties were reviewed. People were sometimes in the position for a year or more before this happened. When it was decided to retain the post the officer who had been acting up all this time had to apply for it along with anyone else who saw the advert. Under normal circumstances you would envisage that the person standing in would have an automatic right to it if they had been doing a satisfactory job. But no – they were interviewed along with the other applicants and on certain notorious instances were not appointed because an outsider scored higher. This completely destroyed the morale of the office. The person who had been doing the job all this time was downgraded to his/her previous post and was expected to train the newcomer about the job that he/she wasn't considered suitable for!

If the situation was reversed it affected people from outside firms applying for the vacancy. They had to ask for a reference beforehand, which may hold them back if their employer thought that they were looking for other work. One attending an interview realised that she was only there to make up numbers as someone was already doing the job.

I'm sure that wasn't the intention of anti-discrimination law.

In a private firm salaries are regularly reviewed. Someone who has made a contribution to the company may well receive a pay rise in his or her current job. This creates job satisfaction and encourages the employees to stay. In most posts in local government this is not practicable. Staff are on rigid pay scales. Even if someone loves the work that they do and has no desire to move, if they want to move on they have to apply for other jobs inside or outside the organisation. This forces their post to become vacant and necessitates another batch of applications, short listing and training of the candidate.

The extensive use of email and the internet for communication has had more far reaching effects that most people could have dreamt of. With the majority of homes having at least one computer, emails have replaced that art of letter writing. The simplicity of typing what you want to say and pressing 'send' has wiped out the need to put your letter in an envelope, find a stamp and take in to a pillar box. It is delivered straightaway. Spelling had gone out of the window. The combination of accidental transposition of letters and intentional use of words such as thru, u and cos, as a result of sending text messages, would never have been done in the days of conventional correspondence. If a response is required the whole transaction can be accomplished in half an hour. Previously this might have taken a week.

Bills can be paid by direct debit or on-line. You can go to an appropriate web site to see what you've bought or your telephone calls for the month. Years ago there was the welcoming sight of the postman on his way hoping that he was going to bring you a letter. This delivery has turned into a groan or at best almost total indifference to the receipt of a pile of junk mail. There have become mail outs at increasingly frequent intervals from a variety of charities, mini catalogues for home purchases, insurance companies and credit card providers that have discouraged people from opening them at all.

There has been the sad consequence on the future of post offices. For years now we have been able to buy stamps at a variety of stores. Although they have retained the contract to pay pensions and benefits, increasingly these are paid directly into a bank account. Two of the few residual services have been removed. You can no longer pay your TV licence in these outlets and your road tax can be paid on-line or over the phone where your insurance documents and MOT certificates are automatically checked in seconds. There is even to be a charge for people who wish to pay their water bills, whilst this can be done free of charge at local shops with 'PayPoint' that also allow payment of utility bills, housing, mobile phone top-ups and season tickets for the bus.

The ability to book flights and holidays over the internet has forced dramatic rationalization of travel agents. Home shopping and on-line purchasing is popular but most of us still prefer to partake in this beloved recreation by browsing in the shopping centres.

Like the escalating use of mobile phones, which happened in the space of only a few years, digital photography was to change the face of picture taking. In the 1960s your Brownie camera let you take only eight or twelve holiday snaps. The improvements to 35mm photography had rolls of film with 20 or 36 pictures. For those of us who took colour slides it was never cheap. The cost of the film and inclusive processing was nearly £2 in 1970 rising to about £8 at the millennium. Some manufacturers stopped supplying film for transparencies altogether.

Cards for the earliest digital cameras held no more than a handful of photos. They were for specialist users such as estate agents advertising their properties. Soon memory cards allowed you to store hundreds. After pressing the shutter you could instantly review the picture, delete it if it was not up to scratch and do a retake. As the memory card would probably only be £10 or so, the price was never a prohibitive factor. Photographic shops were quick to adapt to the changes and obtained equipment into which you inserted your card to select the subjects that you wished to print along with the desired size. All this was at a fraction of previous costs.

By now computers had become far more than something that you used in the office at work having turned into a mass home entertainment centre. Digital photos could be loaded directly and stored in appropriate folders that you can conveniently organize into 'albums.' Photos and slides taken via conventional photography can be scanned in. Excellent software enables you to remove blemishes, darken or brighten the images, add titles or embellish then in a variety of ways. Some that had been confined to the scrap heap could be resurrected by way of this trickery.

In previous years the effort to put on a slide show meant sifting through boxes to find the most appropriate and then loading them into cartridges. Now they can be selected and copied into a folder. Narrative can be added and a professional electronic display readily produced by linking a projector to the computer and using Microsoft Power Point.

You could play a CD whilst using the computer or download music to listen to. There was scarcely anything that you could do that didn't involve an element of IT somewhere. Job applications often had to be submitted on-line. Some firms then conducted an oral interview over the telephone as a method of sieving suitable applicants to a more formal second round. They whole area had developed into 'a way of life.' When my wife had been on a catering course the lecturer had told the class that the sessions would include some IT. 'Oh that's excellent' exclaimed an elderly gentleman 'I love a high tea!'

The use of the internet enabled you to do anything that you wanted. Even though I have worked with computers for approaching 40 years I never cease to be amazed when I load 'Google.' You make an entry to find out about something – 'Walking in the Peak District.' In the time that it takes to blink the response comes back about 438,000 results found in 0.28 seconds. Other incredible feats enable you to have encyclopaedias or maps at any scale from most of the world at your fingertips and enable you to translate passages from any language. Whatever your area of interest you are sure to be able to find an inexhaustible supply of information.

Websites such as Yahoo permit you to have your own email address that can be accessed from anywhere. You could reach acquaintances and family in the most remote places.

Facebook allows people to easily set up their own websites showing their friends anywhere their latest photographs and gossip.

Another that has changed the face of advertising has been Ebay. In the past if you had an item for sale the only places where you could publicise it would be in the window of nearby newsagents, supermarkets or advertise it in the local paper. These methods had a limited audience that suddenly became available to the whole country.

Lulu, used here, enables you to create your own books in he format that you require. Blueprints to assess the product before finalising it can be printed for under £10. When you're happy with it the material can be made available on on-line book stores.

Much as I believe that these are fantastic services and open up a whole new sphere to those of us who are less mobile and active than we used to be, I do feel that it is unhealthy that so many school children pass all their time chatting via the internet. Others, when outdoors, seem to spend much of it doing nothing more constructive than hanging about around off-licences or street corners. The practice of groups of youngsters arranging their own amusements seems to have been totally lost. Only too often the words 'There is nothing to do' are heard. The reasons for things going wrong could form a book in itself but the excessive use of the motor vehicle has been a contributor.

One area that has been appallingly handled above all else is that of traffic, transport and parking. In the sixties only a minority of families possessed a car. In fact it's incredible these days that on one instance when I caught the bus outside the Grammar School that many of the Preston North End football team were on the top deck, having boarded at the previous stop to go into town after a training session.

In TV series, such a Z Cars, actors often sat in a stationary police car whilst the scenery behind them moved. They had to - many of them had never learned to drive!

Car ownership increased and everything was done at the expense of others to accommodate it. Many main roads were widened whilst pavements often narrowed. In some cases, residents' gardens, already quite small, were cut back even further. Corners were often rounded making it easier for motorists but forcing pedestrians into a smaller area when waiting to cross the road.

At this time most people had jobs either in a shop or factory within walking or cycling distance of their home or a short bus ride from the town centre. For those folk that worked in large factories outside the town there was a cavalcade of workmen's buses laid on from all parts of the municipality.

As the populace became more affluent and families bought a car the next logical step was to purchase a house at the edge of the town on the fringe of the countryside. New housing estates were cropping up everywhere. At least during this period they were always built with a few accompanying shops included. The journey to work was not an issue. You simply jumped into the car and drove there. The bus was forgotten about and left to the less prosperous to contend with.

Town centres realised that they had to embrace this modern trend. New shopping centres were constructed with a multi-storey car park attached. Surplus ground next to businesses everywhere was invariably turned into a parking area. This later even included the children's play area and swimming baths on Haslam Park.

Site of the former swimming baths on Haslam Park

As increasing numbers of people expected to use their cars for grocery shopping a new phase was the development of out of town supermarkets. In subsequent years green field sites began to crop up everywhere for giant DIY stores, office blocks and shops to supplement those in the town centres. New areas of housing no longer incorporated shops as they were regarded as irrelevant. Some household names such as Mothercare and Halfords moved away from the High Street completely to areas on the outskirts.

At this time no consideration whatsoever was given to the impact of the increased traffic. There had been congestion on the approach roads to the centre but this later could occur on any road miles out of the town as people lived nowhere near their place of work.

The car was used for every journey. People were heard to

say 'I wouldn't know how to catch a bus.' This had a dramatic effect on their children. The familiar walk to school was abandoned in favour of the automobile. Some parents even arrived at school 20 minutes before classes ended so that they could park as near as possible to the gate. Others cluttered residential avenues. When asked why they used their cars to collect their children parents often explained that the roads were too dangerous – a problem that they were helping to cause. There was a noticeable difference in traffic levels on the roads when the schools were on holiday.

At the end of 1973 OPEC countries in the Middle East quadrupled the price of oil. We were told that the era of cheap fuel was over and that power stations should be converted to being coal-fired and public transport usage increased. Even rationing was talked about. Within a year oil prices had subsided. Bus fares rocketed and passengers deserted them in droves. Thirty odd years later we have had the same colossal leap in prices and subsequent drop.

There have been a couple of hiccups along the way but all along the winner was the car. North Sea oil had come on stream and the world appeared to be awash with it.

At the turn of the century matters were being reconsidered. Global warming was becoming apparent, traffic congestion had worsened substantially, North Sea output was starting to decline and the economies of far eastern nations were leaping ahead adding further pressure to oil production.

Added to these concerns was the health of the nation. There was a need to promote cycling to improve people's fitness and to help relieve congestion. A great concern in recent years has been the increasing obesity in children. A contributory factor has been the lack of exercise walking, often being met with a bar of chocolate at school and then sitting watching television as soon as they arrived home.

Only a few years earlier cycling had been regarded as a joke. It was something done by fitness fanatics or eccentric environmentalists and kids in their own neighbourhood until they were old enough to drive. They were often regarded as a pain on a country road that was too narrow to allow them to be overtaken.

The council had been instrumental in helping cause these problems. In the nineteen fifties and sixties there was only parking in the area enclosed between the buildings. About 1968 some old buildings were demolished and replaced by a multi-storey car park for staff. Over the next thirty years acres of houses and factory units were bulldozed to make way for the relentless increase in parking areas for the various council offices.

The colossal amount of land taken up by car parking. This would appear totally contradictory to plans to increase public transport usage, cycling and waking and reduce dependency on the automobile.

In recent years LCC made an attempt to redress some of the earlier policies in an attempt to demonstrate its green credentials. Questionnaires were sent to staff asking about modes of transport, distances travelled and what measures would have to be taken to persuade them to adopt alternatives. In the vast majority of cases nothing would dissuade them away from their cars. Even if they wanted to, the distance to work and location meant that there was no other method of travel. Other meetings were held to gather information from a variety of transport users travelling to different locations.

Some limited improvements had been put in place for cyclists and runners. Showers were provided and new bike stands. However only a few years before when smoking was banned from all offices some of the old cycle stands were actually removed to make space for a smoking room!

The council's policy was to promote the use of public transport, park and ride schemes, walking and cycling wherever possible. A decision was also taken that new appointments would not be entitled to receive a parking permit unless the nature of their post meant that they were an essential car user.

These coincided with the discovery that there were cracks in the structure of the multi-storey car park at County Hall. Its dangerous state meant that it could not be used and that it would have to be demolished. This would have been an ideal opportunity to get to grips with the entire parking situation.

It didn't happen. Instead staff wasted time driving round mopping up any free places whilst essential travellers coming to attend meetings could not find a space. A new office block known as the Hub was built, several miles out of the town. Some groups of staff were relocated here and it was regularly used for meetings, to provide easier parking. There was poor public transport to these premises. This completely contradicted the council's policy to promote alternatives to the car. In fact some of the staff transferred to these offices who might have walked to work in the town centre were now forced to use the car! As if that was not bad enough that building now has its own parking pressures resulting in the slip roads regularly being crammed with vehicles

Spending cuts had forced the County Council to make savings. Two solutions were to close some of the buildings that it owned, to centralise services and bring more staff into others and the other was to bring in charges for car parking. The levels of tariff were set to make it cheaper to use the Park and Ride facilities rather than part at the work place.

The introduction of parking charges could have worked splendidly. Here was the opportunity for the council to show that it was taking the lead to help reduce congestion and promote car sharing and other forms of transport that it had been declaring its intent for years. As well as raising money directly from the income received from drivers, some of the waste ground taken up could be sold off for building. In addition motorists would not be wasting time in the search for a parking place.

Unions opposed the proposals from day 1. Many members of staff decided that rather than pay they would park in streets away from the council buildings. Others decided that this was the spur that they needed to encourage them to cycle to work. This altruism was not matched by the employers. No additional cycle parking was created in anticipation of the increase. In some other offices such as those in East Cliff there was no access whatsoever by public transport.

From the start there were often large numbers of free spaces in the car parks. The option to pay to park was to be extended to members of staff who did not previously have a parking place – encouraging more people to drive in direct contradiction to the council's policy. Negotiations with the trade unions have resulted in parking charges being halved. It is now cheaper than Park and Ride or the local bus, bicycle parking facilities have not improved and despite utterances about huge improvements for cycling within the city centre nothing has happened.

One is led to the conclusion that the entire reason for the imposition of charges was to make money and carry on as before for cars and congestion.

Enormous changes were to take place regarding working practice. Some antiquated conditions prevented the recruitment of staff for key jobs. Flexi-time that had been operating for more than thirty years would provide greater freedom to become more family-orientated such as leaving at 3 pm if required or starting before or after the core hours. This has been tested out in selected areas.

Employees were allowed to reduce their hours if they wished. This was a bonus for those of us approaching retiring age to gradually put in less time rather than working a solid week to all of a sudden working zero hours.

This wouldn't suit everybody but it was nice to know that the option was there.

A revolution to the way of working allowed staff, if their post was suitable, to work from home part or most of the time. There were many conditions attached. Your position had to require needing little or no supervision or managing others. With computers becoming so cheap and broadband readily available a home office was easy to set up. It was ideally suited to those officers who spent a substantial amount of time writing reports, speaking to clients or whose work was web based.

This suited the council admirably. Office space was freed. There was no need to have a permanent desk with a computer. When you did come into the office you would 'hot desk' using one that was spare at the time. The pressure on car parking spaces was removed and a reduction in congestion. With this extra freedom staff tended to voluntarily work more hours. Other officers that spent much of their time visiting sites or clients were told that their car was their office and they were issued with an upright suitcase to carry their laptop, printer and files that was to become their filing cabinet!

From the days when there was just the odd printer around the department 25 years ago, this had risen to there being several in each office. For forty pounds you can now buy one that will print from the computer, photocopy and print photos directly from a memory card.

An audit took place that checked the numbers and locations of printers in every office in the buildings. Many officers had a printer that was only used occasionally on the few times that they were in work. The various models required a miscellany of cartridges.

A ruling was made that the number of printers known as multi-devices would be vastly reduced, to be located in designated places only. One firm would look after the entire contract. This was also to help with the general reduction in paper. Items would be printed only if there was a need. At many meetings items that would have been previously printed and distributed to each participant would be projected onto a screen directly from the computer.

In many cases reports that had previously sent in the post could be accessed directly from web sites to be printed only if required. You soon discovered that if you couldn't easily print everything, you didn't need to.

# 8

# THE FUTURE

Why have I written this book? I have often reminisced with older colleagues during nostalgic moments about days gone by and things that occurred years ago that our younger friends could not believe. Lots of them said that I should put some of my memoirs into print. Now in my late fifties I am amongst the oldest employees here. I have seen great changes over the years.

As you get older the police constables started to look young. Soon their inspectors and doctors began to have a youthful appearance. It's said that you are not old until the pope and the Archbishop of Canterbury appear young! I was once asked 'Do you like getting old?' I replied 'Not really, but when you think about the alternative!'

When you are 20 you are very concerned what people think about you. When you get to 40 you couldn't care less what people think of you. However when you reach 60 people don't think about you!

What is the definition of an old person? Thirty year ago when my grandmother lived in sheltered accommodation the residents were split into two - the young ones and the old ones. The youngsters were those under 80. Perhaps the best answer is 'somebody who is 15 years older than you!'

When folk were in their twenties and thirties they seldom gave a second thought to their pension. In their forties it assumed greater relevance and in their fifties it was the main topic of conversation. Local Government Officers along with many others in the public sector were allowed to retire at 60 and receive a pension. For every full year that you had worked you got an eightieth of your final year's salary and treble that as a lump sum. That has now changed so that existing staff that were born after 1953 will not collect it until they are 65 and the lump sum element will disappear. The age at which you will receive a state pension is to rise to 68 in about twenty years' time. It is hard to conceive what pensions and life in general will be like in say 2070 when babies born this century come to the end of their working lives.

I mentioned at the beginning the resemblance of the offices to a soap opera. With the exception of murder or deliberately driving into a lake almost every story line from Coronation Street must have happened somewhere over the years. Affairs, a couple splitting up the day after they got married, people being fleeced for everything that they possessed by unscrupulous partners, sex changes, the occasional person being detained at Her Majesty's pleasure, a complete swap of careers from computing to taxi driving or becoming youth hostel wardens. There were employees who had spent time in Japanese Prisoner of War camps. At least on gentleman approaching retirement age used to lie back in his chair for a nap each day after lunch.

Some former teachers who couldn't put up with schooling any more trained as programmers. There were belligerent trade union representatives who were the bane of chief officers and staff with every conceivable form of odd behaviour. There were resignations from people who had had enough – often with their line managers. One man I heard about years earlier was carrying a stack of forms along the corridor. He stopped, threw the lot into the air and yelled 'It's only f...ing paper!' He walked out and wasn't heard of again.

We've had disasters over the years – cancers and heart attacks, fires, suicides and officers killed whilst fell walking and in road accidents. There was a heart breaking tale of a member of staff who was so upset about the way that he had been treated that he developed a malignant brain tumour.

That taught me over the years to not let things at work bother you. It was much better to think that you had a job, hopefully that was interesting and you were paid to do it.

Lots of people didn't and were far worse off than you. A better philosophy was to go home and forget about the office until the next day. Get out into the garden, have that round of golf or do those activities that were the reason that you went to work in the first place.

At the interview for this or any other job a popular question was to be asked 'Why do you want to work for the company?' It was very tempting to give a flippant reply 'Ever since I was a child I've wanted to work in local government!' That would have ensured that you weren't appointed! Presumably this was a test to see what you came up with – given that for most people it was so that they could pay the bills. Almost everyone would contribute to and make the best of whatever occupation they happened to end up doing.

Some aspects of the work move complete circle over the years. When greater independence was given to schools in the eighties several became grant maintained where the Local Authority relinquished all control. These were brought back into the fold in 1998. The new city colleges and academies are again autonomous. The collection of results from the colleges of Further Education that was removed from the authority in the early nineties now appears set to be returned within the next couple of years.

What aspects of work have got worse since I started? The lack of social amenities at work, so popular 30 years ago as to be a major contributory factor to making you want to stay. There has been the palaver to appoint staff. Whilst nobody would want to return to the days where you could be appointed because you had a relative working there or you belonged to the lodge, I believe that the procedure could be simplified. Others have been the relentless rise in meetings, appraisals, one-to-ones and away days quite alien to many older employees. Alongside this there are the constant changes and reorganisations that take place in every firm.

To counter these ICT has undoubtedly created more challenges, made much of the work more rewarding and removed some of the drudgery with more flexible working to match individual circumstances.

Some people approaching retirement age had had enough of these deterrents. Often they now had sufficient money on which to live, their sons and daughters had fled the nest and they simply resigned. They might be able to supplement their savings with some part-time working.

I don't regret working here. Hundreds of delightful friends and colleagues have come and gone. Many had exceptionable ability but left due to the lack of prospects if they stayed where they were. I keep in contact with some if only via a Christmas card.

One lady who came to the office to seek advice gave me a wonderful compliment 'Well I don't feel any the worse for speaking with you!'

Many of us wonder what the future holds for local government and education. Is there a better way to improve services to the public without this huge bureaucracy? The main political parties have an agenda for large academies instead of comprehensive schools. Individual tutors may replace the conventional classroom. Much of the work supporting schools is semi-privatised and has to be self-financing. A high proportion of our remaining duties consists of dealing with children who can't or don't access education. They may be vulnerable at home, may speak little English, consistently play truant or have been excluded.

A certainty is that there will be yet more changes in all aspects of life, work, education and technology for someone to write about in 2050.

Finally I would like to thank everyone who has made a contribution, knowingly or inadvertently.

Room A39 in County Hall. A hundred years earlier this was the court room. During the eighties and nineties it was used by District Audit. For two and a half years since 2006 it has been the base of the Data Analysis team in the School Effectiveness Service. That section, along with several others is to move to offices in East Cliff. The room's new occupants are to be from the Environment Directorate.

Next door to the court room was this cell from where prisoners were taken.

Printed in Great Britain
by Amazon